PHILIPPIANS

A New Testament Commentary

Bob Yandian

PHILIPPIANS: A New Testament Commentary

ISBN: 978-1-68031-079-5
© 2016 by Bob Yandian
Bob Yandian Ministries
PO Box 55236
Tulsa, OK 74155
www.bobyandian.com

Published by Harrison House Publishers
Tulsa, OK 74155
www.harrisonhouse.com

19 18 17 16   10 9 8 7 6 5 4 3 2 1

Printed in the United States of America.

Table of Contents

PHILIPPIANS

VERSE BY VERSE COMMENTARY

The personal study notes of BOB YANDIAN

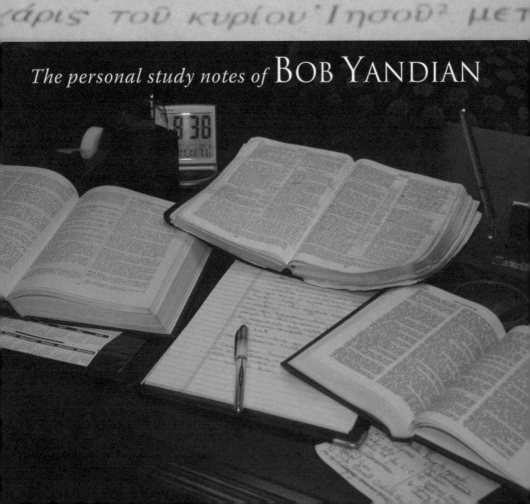

Introduction

My heart echoes a statement Peter made in his last epistle:

For this reason I will not be negligent to remind you always of these things, though you know and are established in the present truth.

2 Peter 1:12

The "for this reason" was to build on his previous statement — Peter's desire for all believers not just to get to heaven, but to have an abundant entrance into heaven. A working knowledge and practice of the Word of God is necessary for an abundant entrance, which is marked by rewards and rulership.

In order to establish that abundant entrance, Peter taught believers what they should know again and again, "though you know them." What was taught them was the present truth. The present truth is what was being written in the day of the apostles Peter, Paul, John, and James.

This present truth is what believers still need to be gloriously saved. The Old Testament is to be studied in the light of the New Testament epistles. The four gospels are to be studied in the light of the New Testament epistles. Not only should every Christian know the epistles, they should be established in them.

This is why I have written this series of books, verse-by-verse teachings on the epistles of Paul, Peter, John, and James. This is truly meat for our time period, our dispensation: the Church Age.

Bob Yandian
Author

Introduction

Philippians Overview

Writer: The Apostle Paul.

Time: About 61–66 AD.

Occasion: Paul was under house arrest in Rome. He was writing to the town where he and Silas were imprisoned for the first time (Acts 16). Paul is expressing his thanks and appreciation to the group of people who stood by him with their prayers and financial support. This church had done more than any other.

While Paul was under house arrest, he was always chained to a guard. Many of his guards accepted the Lord, and Paul will tell of their greetings from Nero's house (Philippians 4:22).

Theme: Joy (*chara*) in the midst of every situation. Paul suffered imprisonment, yet he had joy. This joy is above and beyond what the world can have or understand (4:7).

Background on Philippi

Situated on the level plain where the battle took place between the combined forces of Antony and Brutus and those of Cassius and Octavius. In honor of the battle, the Romans made it a colony and a border garrison — an outpost for Caesar. Because of the city's great beauty, it became a retirement center for Roman military personnel. The Philippian people were very disciplined and understood authority. There was no synagogue in Philippi because there were no Jews there that we know of.

Historical Background (Acts 15:36–16:12)

In verse 36 of Acts 15, Paul asked Barnabas to return to Galatia and visit the churches in that region. There had just been a counsel in Jerusalem to discuss various areas of legalism toward Gentile churches. The church at Jerusalem was still considered to be the governing church (Galatians 2:1–10). The "doubtful things of Corinth" (liberties enjoyed by Gentiles) were discussed. Compromises in convictions were made so believers could work together. These were also agreed on between Jews and Gentiles as proper submission to authority (15:21). Paul needed to return to the churches he had established and give them direction. Barnabas again wanted to take Mark (15:37–38), who had deserted them in Pamphylia on the first missionary journey (13:13). Paul calls him a deserter and lazy because he would not work.

Barnabas and Paul got into an argument (15:39–41). It was difficult for Barnabas to become angry enough to confront Paul. He is called the "son of consolation" (exhortation and encouragement) (4:36). He was among those who gave in to the legalistic Jews in Galatians 2:13 ". . . insomuch that Barnabas also was carried away."

Barnabas was right concerning the issue, but wrong in getting angry. Barnabas erred against authority and Paul erred against grace. Barnabas should have submitted to Paul, and Paul should have submitted to the grace of God. This was the attack of Satan to destroy the work in Galatia, but it did not work. Paul went one way with Silas, while Barnabas went another way with Mark, and God blessed them all.

In Acts, chapter 16, verses 1 and 2, Paul and Silas found Timothy in Galatia. He was a disciple raised by a believing mother and grandmother (2 Timothy 1:5). His unbelieving father had deserted him at a young age. Timothy had a good reputation with the saints in Galatia, and Paul wanted him on his team.

In verse 3, Paul had Timothy circumcised. He would be working around Jews, and it was important to have him circumcised. Titus was not circumcised (Galatians 2:3) because his ministry was around Gentiles, and it would be a matter of legalism to do so.

There is a time when something is right and a time when it is wrong. These issues are not spelled out in the Word of God, and a person has to know how to "discern between good and evil" (Hebrews 5:14). Wrong decisions concerning such things can result in barriers which hinder witnessing and missionary work.

In verse 4, Paul took the decrees from the Jerusalem church to these Gentile churches and established them in submission to the authority of the apostles and elders. Acts 16:5 shows this stabilized the churches in Galatia.

Paul would never come into a city and demand change of the Gentiles before preaching the gospel to them. He became all things to all men. However, after they accepted salvation, changes were imposed, and the believers submitted for peace and the furtherance of the gospel.

In verses 6 through 8, the Holy Spirit forbade Paul to go to Bithynia and Asia but Paul kept on moving until he came to Troas, a city on the Aegean Sea.

God gave Paul a vision to go to Macedonia, so he and his team launched out (vv. 9–10). The winds were perfect to send them straight there. Notice the order of events: Paul was always on the go for the Lord, and he received a vision. Then circumstances lined up. Circumstances will line up after a call, but we do not necessarily have a call just because circumstances line up.

The man in Paul's vision came from Philippi, a Roman colony, so Paul began his work there. Philippian citizens had the same laws, rights, and privileges of Rome. Later, when Paul was arrested, his Roman citizenship would come in handy (v. 12).

1:1–30 The Joy of Sharing the Sufferings of Christ

The Challenge of Chapter One

Our response to suffering will be a witness to the reality of Jesus Christ. Jesus sets the example for us to follow: His response to undeserved suffering for righteousness sake at the Cross led both the repentant thief and the Roman centurion to salvation.

As the apostle Paul witnessed the sufferings of Stephen being stoned to death for his faith in Jesus, it made an impact on his life. In turn, Paul's attitude toward suffering has been a witness to many.

The power of the Christian life must be left in the realm of the Spirit and grace. It cannot be reduced to a system of dos and don'ts, but must be continued as a personal relationship with Jesus Christ.

Christ is the visible image of God (who is invisible), and He created everything in both heaven and earth. It is through Him that all things created are held together. We are the body of Christ, and He is the Head of the Church. We were once separated from God, but through the shed blood of Jesus, we have been reconciled to Him. We are admonished to continue in the truth of the Word because it is through the Word operating in our lives that we have hope for the future.

I. Entering into the Sufferings of Christ (1–11)

Serving the Lord brings blessings, but it also brings the opposition of Satan.

> **1:1 ¶ Paul and Timothy, bondservants of Jesus Christ, ¶ To all the saints in Christ Jesus who are in Philippi, with the bishops and deacons:**

Paul and Timotheus (Timothy) the servants (*doulos*: bond slaves) of Jesus Christ . . .

Paul and Timothy were voluntary slaves to the Lord Jesus. The Roman Empire had millions of slaves, so this term was well known to the Philippian people.

Each believer has the choice of slavery to Christ. They can choose to lay down their own plans and operate in their spiritual office thus building up the Church. No church can operate on the offices of only one or two people. It takes teamwork among many believers functioning in their offices to operate a church.

. . . to all the saints (*hagios*: holy, sanctified ones) in Christ Jesus

"In Christ Jesus" is where we are as saints. This is our spiritual location and divine viewpoint for life. Paul made it his daily vantage point and encourages us to make it ours as well.

. . . which are at Philippi

These believers are in Christ and at Philippi. We live in two worlds: the spiritual and the natural. This will be amplified in chapter 3, verse 20.

. . . with the bishops (*episkopos*: overseers)

These were the pastors of the churches at Philippi. They carried the authority over the churches to teach and preach the Word of God to the people. As apostles, Paul and Timothy spoke first to those in authority in the churches: the pastors, bishops, and guardians.

. . . and deacons (*diakonos*: servers, workers)

Finally, Paul addresses those who serve from the congregation. No church can be successful without a proper chain of command. Paul knows the chain of command which exists in their local church and he addresses it. From this verse on, Paul will not mention authority. The Philippians understood authority, and Paul never had to use the term "apostle." This is the only book Paul wrote (except for Hebrews) in which he did not mention his office. From this point on, Paul writes in the first person using "I" instead of "we" in addressing the saints. Although Timothy was present with him, the rest of this letter was from Paul only.

A. Grace: Where It All Begins

1:2 ¶ Grace to you and peace from God our Father and the Lord Jesus Christ.

Grace (*charis*) be unto you and peace (*eirene*)...

This grace is not saving grace but living grace. It is multiplied to us through knowledge of the Word of God (2 Peter 1:2) and also increases peace to us. This grace comes through an increase of faith and is called "more grace" (James 4:6). All of this is in the subjunctive mood which indicates that such grace is potential. Peace is the result of reconciliation (Ephesians 2:14–17).

. . . from God our Father, and from the Lord Jesus Christ.

This half of the verse emphasizes the source of grace and peace: it is not human but divine. It will exceed anything we can imagine or understand (4:7). Grace summarized the plan of God, and peace is the result of our entrance into that plan.

The next few verses show the progression of God's plan. Our Christian life begins with the new birth, develops through prayer, followed by participation in ministry. This results in spiritual growth and an increase of grace until we finally attain spiritual maturity.

B. Prayer: Our Power in the Midst of Suffering

1:3 ¶ I thank my God upon every remembrance of you,

1. Background: Paul's Attitude Toward the Philippians

The epistle to the Philippians is the most personal letter Paul wrote. The saints at Philippi were closer to him than any other group as is brought out in other parts of the letter:

> a) Paul is filled with joy at every remembrance of the Philippians (3–4).
>
> b) Paul is filled with confidence at their spiritual growth (5–6).
>
> c) Paul longs to see the Philippian believers (7–8).
>
> d) Paul has such a burden for the Philippians that he would rather stay and work for them than die and be with the Lord (23, 25).
>
> e) His attitude toward the Philippians is one of rejoicing (2:2).
>
> f) He considers the Philippians to be his "joy and crown" (4:1).

2. Word Study: Remembrance

> a) Remembrance toward the Lord brings stability and inner happiness (Psalm 145:7–10, Ecclesiastes 12:1).

b) The Lord's Supper is designed to bring us to remembrance of Him (Luke 22:19–20; 1 Corinthians 11:23–25).

c) Mature believers leave remembrances for others (Proverbs 10:7, Philippians 1:3).

d) Remembrance of the Word is a top priority of life (2 Peter 1:12–13).

e) Remembrance of the Word brings security to the believer during the worst of persecution (Psalm 119:16, 82, 93, 109, 141).

f) Rememberance of sin, discipline, and apostasy leave only unhappy memories (Lamentations 3:16–24).

1:4 always in every prayer of mine making request for you all with joy,

Always in every prayer (*deesis*: supplication) of mine for you all making request (*deesis*) with joy (*chara*),

Not only is Paul supplicating before the Father, but the Philippians are the subject of those prayers. In all of the prayers Paul makes before the Lord, the Philippians are mentioned in them. When Paul prays for them, there is never a note of urgency or despondency but always of joy. To pray for someone or something, they have to come to your mind. Whenever the Philippians came to Paul's mind, joy accompanied the thought.

3. Insights into Paul's Prayer Life

a) Paul's prayer was motivated by an attitude of thankfulness.

b) It was based on the knowledge of God's Word. Prayer is an extension of the study of Scriptures. No one can study the Word all day long, but you can apply what you have learned from your studies throughout the day, long after the pages of your Bible have been closed.

c) Foundations for prayer

1) Knowledge of appropriate Scripture

2) Faith

3) Freedom from sin

4) Grace orientation

5) Mastery of the circumstances of life (4:11–12)

6) Attitude of rest (4:6–7)

7) Love toward God, spouse, believers, and unbelievers

d) The fundamentals of answered prayer (found in James 5:16–18, 1 John 5:14–15).

C. Partnership Brings a Share of the Victories

1:5 for your fellowship in the gospel from the first day until now,

For your fellowship (*koinonia*: joint participation, partnership) in the gospel from the first day until now,

This is the reason for Paul's joy. The Philippians have been faithful partners with him in the ministry of the gospel. Paul has gone through the worst of circumstances (2 Corinthians 4:7–15, 11:23–33), and the Philippians have stood with him. Their fellowship has been a source of great strength during these times. This is why joy comes to him whenever he thinks of them.

1. The Philippians were partners with Paul in the ministry of the gospel (1:5).

2. Partnership includes grace (1:7), rewards, and blessings. Their prayer and financial support allowed them to share in Paul's victories.

3. Partnership is being like-minded (2:1–2).

4. Partnership gives power for daily life (3:10).

5. Partnership includes financial support for the ministry (4:15).

D. Spiritual Growth Follows Prayer and Partnership

1:6 being confident of this very thing, that He who has begun a good work in you will complete *it* until the day of Jesus Christ;

Being confident (*peitho*: persuaded) of this very (specific) thing . . .

This confidence and persuasion comes from the knowledge of the Word of God ("we are always confident, knowing," 2 Corinthians 5:6).

... that he which hath begun a good (*agathos*) work in you ...

The "good work" is God's plan for our lives which was started at the new birth. This plan includes daily maturity in the Word and divine production (witnessing, laying on of hands, etc.). Paul emphasizes that it is God the Father who begins this good work in us.

... will perform (*epiteleo*: conclude, complete) it until the day of Jesus Christ;

The "day" is the rapture, the resurrection of the Church.

God will continue to complete His work in each believer until the day Jesus returns.

1:7 just as it is right for me to think this of you all, because I have you in my heart, inasmuch as both in my chains and in the defense and confirmation of the gospel, you all are partakers with me of grace.

Even as it is (only) meet (*dikaios*: right, just) for me to think this of you all, because I have you in my heart ...

Paul considers every believer in Philippi to be his partner and he holds each of them in his heart.

Of all the churches Paul started, the Philippian congregation is the most mature. Paul speaks of them as living sacrifices. The potential sins mentioned in this book are sins of maturity which stem from arrogance (3:13–16).

... in as much as both in my bonds (prison) and in the defense (*apologia*: the defense of our beliefs) and confirmation (*bebeias*) of the gospel ...

Paul defends the gospel to those who resists. He confirms it to those who are open and positive toward the Word of God.

The Greek word *apologia* is where we get the English word "apologetics." It is translated "defense" and "answer" in a number of passages (Acts 19:33, 22:1, 24:10, 25:16, 1 Corinthians 9:3, Philippians 1:7, 17, 2 Timothy 4:16, 1 Peter 3:15).

We do not defend the Word but use it to defend our cause. Nor do we apologize for our beliefs. Rather, we have important information and defend what we know to be true.

E. Five Goals of Apologetics

1. The goal of our defense is a change of mind or repentance. The purpose of witnessing is to cause the mind of an unbeliever to change toward Christ, not for us to win an argument.

2. The unbeliever must understand that a Holy God exists and he, a sinner, is unacceptable to a Holy God.

3. The discussion should stress the difference between God, the Creator, and man, the creature.

4. The fall of man separated righteous God from unrighteous man.

5. The unbeliever must face the plan of God which is grace and God's ultimate victory based on the finished work of the Cross.

F. Growth Starts with an Increase of Grace

. . . ye all are partakers (*sugkoinonos*) of my grace.

Paul and his partners, the Philippians, first share in the grace of God poured out on Paul in prison, then grow and partake of "more grace" (Romans 8:32, James 4:6).

1:8 For God is my witness, how greatly I long for you all with the affection of Jesus Christ.

For God is my record (*martus*: witness, record) how greatly I long (strongly desire) after you all in the bowels (*splagchnon*: deep emotions, compassion, inward affection) of Jesus Christ.

The Greek word *martus* is where we get the English word "martyr." The meaning has evolved from "one who tells or records what he has seen" to "one who willingly suffers death or torture rather than renounce his beliefs."

In this verse, Paul uses it in the classic sense of bearing witness. The Lord Himself has been called to witness Paul's intense desire to visit the Philippians after his release from prison.

Paul will do this a number of times throughout this book, demonstrating his true feelings and accountability to the Philippians.

F. More Grace Results in Much Fruit

1:9 ¶ And this I pray, that your love may abound still more and more in knowledge and all discernment,

And this I pray (*proseuchomai*: continuous praying), that your love (*agape*) may abound yet more and more (in overflowing) in knowledge (*epignosis*) and in all judgment (*aesthesis*: discernment),

Paul's prayer, offered continuously, is that the Philippians will also enter into apologetics, the defense of the gospel. First, he prayed for the overflowing of love in their lives. The primary goal of witnessing is to let the unbeliever see the love of God emanating from our lives.

Next, Paul prays they will have knowledge and discernment. The unbeliever needs to see that we have keen discernment toward the realities of life. This is formed in our lives by a great knowledge of the Word of God.

Both knowledge and love are essential. If knowledge is not mixed with love in our lives, we will become arrogant (1 Corinthians 8:1).

1:10 that you may approve the things that are excellent, that you may be sincere and without offense till the day of Christ,

(So) [t]hat ye may approve (*dokimazo*: test) things that are excellent (superior); that ye may be sincere (*heilikrines*: examine in sunlight, genuine) and without offence (*aproskopos*: a stumbling block) till the day of Christ

The purpose of witnessing and having the Word with love in our lives is so the unbeliever can see we are genuine and have an excellence in our lives that is supernatural.

Wine, when it is being tested for true quality, is held up to the light. Our lives are held up before sinners — they can tell if we are hypocrites or not.

In the next verse, these virtues will be called "fruits." These things in our lives will be used by the Holy Spirit to pierce the hearts (Acts 2:37) of those we are witnessing to. However, if we have sin in our lives and are truly hypocrites before them, we become a stumblingblock to their receiving the Lord as Savior.

1:11 being filled with the fruits of righteousness which *are* by Jesus Christ, to the glory and praise of God.

Being filled (*pleroo*) with the fruits (production, evidence) of righteousness...

We are filled with the production of righteousness by being filled with the knowledge of the Word. This knowledge, mixed with love, causes works to be seen. Then the world knows we are genuine.

. . . which are (come) by Jesus Christ, unto the glory and praise of God.

This is the same Lord who began the good work in us and will also perfect or complete it (v. 6). He is called the author and finisher (completer) of our faith (Hebrews 12:2). Our witness begins with the new birth in our own lives, progresses with the intake of the Word and the growth of love, and finally yields the production of fruit to the world. In all of this, Jesus Christ enables us, and God the Father receives all of the glory.

II. The Spiritually Mature Believer in Suffering (12–26)

These verses first discuss suffering caused by personal choice which is accompanied by divine discipline. Then Paul deals with a higher form of suffering — suffering caused by our environment — which is under the control of the god of this world, Satan.

1:12 ¶ But I want you to know, brethren, that the things *which happened* to me have actually turned out for the furtherance of the gospel,

But I would ye should understand (want you to learn), brethren . . .

Paul's express desire in prison was that the saints in Philippi would learn something which would benefit their lives. Circumstances in life are designed by God to be opportunities to advance our knowledge of the plan of God. Faith used during trials causes our confidence to be built up and our anticipation of future blessings to become greater. The Philippians are concerned about Paul's well-being, and Paul is concerned about their knowledge of the plan of God for their own lives.

A. Seeing God's Plan Behind Circumstances

. . . that the things (circumstances) which happened unto me have fallen out (turned out by divine decree) rather unto the furtherance (*prokope*: to cut ahead, advancement, progress) of the gospel.

Prokope is a Greek military term for the soldiers who cut through the brush to pave the way for the advancing army behind them.

B. Historical Background

Paul was out of the will of God when he went to Jerusalem. However, he confessed his sin in jail in Caesarea and is now back in God's will.

He has been taken to Rome and has spent five years getting back to the place God wanted him to be. Now that he is coming to the end of his prison sentence, he sees that these things have turned out for the "furtherance" of the gospel of the Lord. Paul has been "cutting through the brush" while in prison to pave the way for the saints in Philippi and the rest of the Body of Christ. The gospel has progressed even though Paul is in chains.

Paul kept an attitude of inner happiness while suffering with the Lord, and it made an impact on those around him.

> **1:13 so that it has become evident to the whole palace guard, and to all the rest, that my chains are in Christ;**

So that my bonds in Christ are manifest in (among) all the palace (*praitoron*: palace guards), and in all other places (citizens of Rome);

Not only was Paul chained to a Roman guard at all times, but a Roman guard was chained to Paul. The greater influence was not from the guard to Paul, but from Paul to the guard.

The fact that Paul was a believer and a minister of the Lord Jesus was now well known to the prison guard unit and to the citizens of Rome. Although Paul was small in stature compared to the Roman soldiers he was chained to, he was never intimidated. He declared war against the god of the Roman Empire and, one by one, began to win guards to the Lord Jesus.

During Paul's two years in jail, many guards had been saved and filled with the Holy Spirit, and had committed their families also to the Lord. This had spilled over from their families to the general population of Rome, and

Paul was now famous.

Daily, members of our own congregations are "bound" to people on the job, in the schools, etc., and never mention Jesus to them. Paul was a great example of making the best out of every situation and turning every opportunity into a chance to witness.

1:14 and most of the brethren in the Lord, having become confident by my chains, are much more bold to speak the word without fear.

And many of the brethren in the Lord, waxing confident (*peitho*: courageous) by (because of) my bonds, are much more bold (*tolmao*: confident) to speak the word without fear.

Other ministers are looking at Paul and receiving confidence to preach the Word. When Paul was first put in prison, they were concerned for their own safety and were afraid to preach. They did not want to be known as ministers of the gospel.

But as Paul stays in prison year after year, and remains bold to preach and write, their fear is changed to courage. Paul's boldness to witness to his guards causes many other ministers to rise up in boldness and preach the Word without fear of what men and governments might do to them. Thus, Paul's prison term is used by the Lord to further the gospel by turning timid preachers into bold ones.

Also, many of the churches have become legalistic and inwardly focused. They are caught up in putting more laws, rules, and regulations on the people. When they see the fruit Paul is bearing even while going through such persecution, they realize the only important thing is the Word, and they rise up to preach it with boldness.

Many of the ministers in the cities across Macedonia are preaching to be recognized. They are looking for better sermons to impress their own people and other ministers. Paul wakes them up to realize that the only one who needs to be impressed with our lifestyle and ministry is the Lord Jesus. Because Paul did not care if he was known, he became known. If ministers will be content to preach where God has called them and not try to be seen of men, they will be known in the right places (Luke 2:52).

C. Paul's Attitude Toward Those Who Cause Suffering

1:15 ¶ Some indeed preach Christ even from envy and strife, and some also from goodwill:

Some indeed (Why should some) preach Christ even of envy (*phthonos*: jealousy) and strife (*eris*: rivalry); and some also of good will (*eudokia*: delight):

Paul's message has become a major dividing point between Jewish believers, Gentile believers, and false teachers. Now some are using the pulpit as nothing more than a means to defend their views and ridicule Paul's.

The pulpit is a sacred place, and God holds teachers of the Word more accountable than other Christians (James 3:1). The pulpit is to be used to minister salvation to the sinner and teach the Word to the believer. There may be times to inform the people against false teaching circulating in your city which is not in line with the Word and traditionally accepted beliefs, but this situation does not happen too often.

In these verses, Paul is not so much addressing what is being said as he is—the attitude behind it. Motivation behind the preaching is more important than the content, and in the churches of Rome, ministers are preaching the gospel out of wrong motives (15–18).

Some are preaching the gospel out of strife and jealousy toward Paul, while others are preaching out of love for the people and the truth.

Good will and love are the best attitudes to minister with. Love cares for the people, not the minister's beliefs or personal doctrines. Anyone who ministers out of strife and rivalry is more concerned with himself than the congregation.

These men are jealous of Paul's success. He has succeeded where they have failed, and they hate him for it. They now talk evil of him from the pulpit and pick apart his doctrines. They believe that since he is in prison, he cannot defend himself. They do not realize they are not hurting him at all; they are only hurting themselves.

1:16 The former preach Christ from selfish ambition, not sincerely, supposing to add affliction to my chains;

The one (Some on one hand) preach Christ of contention (*eritheia*: self-promotion), not sincerely, supposing to add affliction to my bonds:

Some are using their pulpit to add insult to injury in Paul's life. They not only want Paul to stay in prison, but for him to be miserable, too. They did not want him to experience joy while there. They have supposed falsely that while they are preaching in contention, Paul is being hurt by their words, but they are wrong and only fooling themselves.

The Greek word translated "contention" comes from a root word meaning "someone who is a hired laborer." These people are preaching the gospel mainly for money. Paul's message of grace and his success have become a threat to them.

These men are out to build their ministry on the destruction of another. Their motivation is hatred and jealousy toward the success Paul has achieved despite his circumstances. Paul may have been in prison bodily in Rome, but these ministers were in prison in their souls.

1:17 but the latter out of love, knowing that I am appointed for the defense of the gospel.

But the other (some on the other hand) of (out of) love (*agape*), knowing (*oida*: understanding) that I am set (appointed) for the defence (*apologia*) of the gospel.

Other ministers love both the gospel and Paul. These people know that Paul is in prison as a buffer for the gospel, sent there to stop the opposition at its source: the Roman courts of Caesar. They are preaching the gospel for the people's sake, not their own. Their motives and attitudes are pure before the Lord and they, like Paul, are free in their souls.

1:18 What then? Only that in every way, whether in pretense or in truth, Christ is preached; and in this I rejoice, yes, and will rejoice.

What then (what is the solution)? Notwithstanding, every way (by any mode or method), whether in pretence (*prophasis*: hypocrisy), or in truth, Christ is preached; and I therein do rejoice, yea, and will rejoice.

Paul's solution is to cast his burden on the Lord and not to worry about what men were doing to his doctrines and reputation. Even though there were ministers tearing him apart in their pulpits, stealing his revelations (and preaching them as their own), and setting themselves up as the standard before the people, Paul was not going to be concerned. Their hypocrisy does not cause Paul to lose one moment of sleep.

Paul was rejoicing that perhaps someone would come to know the Lord as Savior in their meetings. In this he did rejoice and would continue to do so.

1:19 ¶ For I know that this will turn out for my deliverance through your prayer and the supply of the Spirit of Jesus Christ,

For I know that this shall turn to my salvation (*soteria*: deliverance) through your prayer, and the supply of the Spirit of Jesus Christ,

Paul has prayed for the Philippians (v. 4), and now they are praying for him.

This verse demonstrates Paul's application of Romans 8:28: "And we know that all things work together for good to them that love God, to them who are the called according to his purpose." Though Paul is being maligned and blasted from the pulpits of Rome, God is going to turn around the situation through the prayers of the saints from all over the world and by the power of the Holy Spirit. God always vindicates honor and integrity.

Paul saw every event, whether for or against him, as an opportunity for the gospel to be spread. In his lifetime, the gospel was taken to an area larger than the United States. It all occurred because of the dedication of this one man.

Paul did not live for the Lord only in church or at home. He lived for the Lord and the preaching of the gospel wherever he was. He also used every opportunity — whether free or in prison, in church or at home, in the city or country — as a chance to preach the gospel. He accomplished much through his preaching, his lifestyle, and his prayers as well as the prayers of those who stood with him.

D. Magnifying Christ in Every Situation

1:20 according to my earnest expectation and hope that in nothing I shall be ashamed, but with all boldness, as always, so now also Christ will be magnified in my body, whether by life or by death.

According to my earnest expectation and my hope, that in nothing I shall be ashamed (*aischunomai*: disgraced), but that with all boldness, as always, so now also Christ shall be magnified (*megaluno*: exalted) in my body, whether it be by life, or by death.

Paul's expectation and hope are for the gospel to be spread and for many to come to know the Lord as savior. Paul's expectation and hope are also for those who are saved to come to the full knowledge of the truth and grow into maturity.

Nothing will stop this from happening: men may preach against him and use him as the object of ridicule, he may be imprisoned or martyred, but nothing will stop the gospel from being preached or the Word from being taught.

Paul will never be put to shame. He will continue to preach the gospel in all boldness because his confidence is not in men but in the living God. With this attitude, Jesus will be magnified in every situation Paul goes through whether good or bad.

Paul's attitude in suffering or prosperity was to see to it that Christ was magnified. When we place our lives in the Lord's keeping and realize nothing can defeat us, we will always come out on top, and Jesus will be magnified through our lives in the eyes of others.

This is the height of the life of witnessing. If we speak or act, Jesus Christ is magnified. If we live or die, sink or swim, Jesus Christ is magnified. People then have no control over our lives. If we prosper and people praise us, pride cannot enter in and affect us. If we are in harsh times and going through persecution, their antagonism cannot destroy us, because we realize God is going to be glorified.

This brings joy into every situation. We cannot save or keep ourselves and we do not need to try. By simply trusting the Lord in each situation, we remain at rest and detached from the circumstances of life (4:11–13). Paul is not bound by people nor the details of life. He is only consumed with glorifying the Lord Jesus Christ in any situation of life or even death.

1:21 For to me, to live *is* Christ, and to die *is* gain.

Paul's whole life is dedicated to the Lord. To live each day is Christ, and if death is to come, he considers it a promotion. Paul does not say, "To live is possessions, pleasure, pleasing people, and the praise of others." All these things are fine if they come, otherwise he will not concern himself with them.

To live on the earth brings glory to the Lord and to die brings glory to the believer. In either case, possessions, popularity or power are not glorified or sought after. Rather, we seek God, and all we need will be provided (Psalm 37:4, Matthew 6:33).

Paul's desire in living is to be a servant and display the character of Christ. As Paul tells of the labors of Epaphroditus (2:30), we see his team shared the same vision of ministry.

1:22 But if *I* live on in the flesh, this *will mean* fruit from *my* labor; yet what I shall choose I cannot tell.

But if I live (on) in the flesh, this is the fruit (production) of my labour: yet what I shall choose I wot (know) not.

If Paul were to live longer on the earth, he would continue to produce fruit through those he ministers to. His fruit would be Christ. The longer he lives, the more opportunity he has to reveal the Lord to those he comes into contact with.

Paul does not know right now which choice he will make. He could stay and reflect Jesus Christ, or he could die and have an abundant entrance into the everlasting kingdom of the Lord Jesus Christ (2 Peter 1:11). We know his answer will be to stay because Paul did not die at this time, but lived on for several more years and wrote several other epistles. (His last letter was 2 Timothy.)

1:23 For I am hard-pressed between the two, having a desire to depart and be with Christ, *which is* far better.

For I am in a straight betwixt two (*sunecho*: hard-pressed from two directions) having a desire to depart (*analuo*: strike the tent, break camp), and to be with Christ; which is far better (more preferable).

Paul, a tent maker, uses a military term for striking a tent, leaving one camp, and heading toward another. The tent Paul is speaking of is his body (2 Peter 1:14). He would be leaving his body and going from earth to heaven to be face-to-face with the Lord. Right then, if he had been given his choice, he would have preferred to go to heaven and be with the Lord.

However, he knows there is more to be done, and his work with the Philippians is not over.

1:24 Nevertheless to remain in the flesh *is* more needful for you.

Every minister comes to a point where he wants to give up and go on to be with the Lord. Paul has come to that point.

Yet, there are two overriding factors which enter in. First, the will of God must always be the top priority; God's will for Paul at this time is to continue on in the ministry. Second is the need of the people. The heart cry of a true minister is for the need of the people God has called him to. Paul puts his own desires second to the needs of the Philippians.

1:25 And being confident of this, I know that I shall remain and continue with you all for your progress and joy of faith,

And having this confidence (being persuaded of this), I know that I shall abide (*meno*: remain) and continue with (*sumparameno*: stay beside) you all . . .

The struggle between two pressing forces is over and there is no more debating in Paul's mind. Paul will not only remain on the earth (*meno*) but will also stay beside (*sumparameno*) the Philippian people.

The word *meno* is the root of both words. Paul will remain on the earth, but he could be in any location. Yet, he will always be with the Philippian people since they are in his heart.

. . . for your furtherance (*prokope*: advancement) and joy of (in the) faith,

Paul will stay on the earth because the Word is not yet complete (Colossians 1:25). Paul has much more to write and minister. In so doing, not only will the Philippian people advance and increase in joy, but so will we today.

Joy in the faith is joy in the Word of God. "The faith" is a technical word for God's Word. Advancement in the Word of God is the fundamental reason God leaves us here on the earth.

We do not need to seek joy, it will come as we advance in spiritual maturity. Joy is a fruit of the recreated human spirit (Galatians 5:22). Fruit does not try to grow, but grows naturally when the conditions of light and water are present. Joy will come naturally in our life when the conditions of the Word, prayer, and spiritual advancement are met.

1:26 that your rejoicing for me may be more abundant in Jesus Christ by my coming to you again.

That your rejoicing (*kauchema*: reason of boasting) may be more abundant (*perisseuo*: overflowing) in Jesus Christ for me by my coming (*parousia*: arrival, presence) to you again.

The Philippian people have had rejoicing before with Paul and his team (Acts 16). There was great joy when the church was begun at the home of Lydia. Rejoicing also came when the girl with the spirit of divination was delivered and the Philippian jailer was saved along with his family.

The team which stayed behind when Paul went on to Thessalonica and Berea helped establish the church and the believers. Because of this, revival broke out and many came to know the Lord and be established in the Word and the local churches.

Yet, Paul knows that their spiritual advancement was not yet complete, and there was more he had to do for them.

Now that Paul is planning to come back again, their rejoicing will be overflowing more than ever before.

III. The Partnership of Suffering (27–30)

The third section concerns the highest form of suffering: suffering caused by our stand for Christ or suffering for righteousness sake (Matthew 5:10–12, 1 Peter 4:12–19).

1:27 ¶ Only let your conduct be worthy of the gospel of Christ, so that whether I come and see you or am absent, I may hear of your affairs, that you stand fast in one spirit, with one mind striving together for the faith of the gospel,

Only (Now that I am remaining with you) let your conversation (*politeuomai*: responsibility as a citizen) be as it becometh (weighs heavily in the direction of) the gospel of Christ . . .

Our word for "politics" comes from the word *politeuomai*. In choosing this word, Paul is making an analogy between being good citizens of Rome and good citizens of heaven.

Philippi, a Roman colony, had all the privileges of Rome. A Roman citizen felt at home in the city. The born-again believer is in a colony of heaven called earth. The believer is a citizen of heaven and has all of the rights and privileges of the streets of gold. We are not to take advantage of this before others but to live reverently, knowing our lifestyle can influence others to receive Jesus as their own Savior.

The word picture Paul uses here is of weighing something on scales; living a godly life before the world tips the unbeliever's scale toward the gospel of Jesus Christ.

. . . that whether I come and see you, or else be absent, I may hear of your affairs, that ye stand fast (*steko*: hold your ground) in one spirit (vision) with one mind (*psuche*: soul) striving (contending as a team of athletes) together for the faith of (namely) the gospel.

The prayer of every minister is that his people will live for the Lord, whether he himself is present or absent, and whether he is successful or unsuccessful in living the Christian life (2 Corinthians 13:9).

If Paul had gone on to be with the Lord during this time of pressure in his life, his prayer would be that the saints at Philippi would continue to live for the Lord and hold fast to the ground they have claimed. Their unity of Spirit teamed up with their unity of mind would have enabled them to live for the gospel like a team of athletes contending for a victory crown. With a common goal of living for Christ, they would have rallied around the Word of God, the faith.

Every pastor's desire is for the people to continue the work after he dies or else is called by God to another place. The people may miss him, but they know the Lord is always there and God can supply another pastor. They do not live for the Lord only because the pastor is present, but because Jesus Himself is there.

Once this principle is understood, the believer will work harder on the job. He will not work because the boss is present, but because the Lord is present (Ephesians 6:5–8). The wife will be more productive in the house. She will work because the Lord is present whether her husband is there or not.

1:28 and not in any way terrified by your adversaries, which is to them a proof of perdition, but to you of salvation, and that from God.

And in nothing terrified (*pturomenoi*: frightened by nothing) by your adversaries (*antikeimai*: those entrenched in opposition toward you) . . .

This phrase is from the analogy of a timid horse facing battle. The word was also used in the city to describe the suicide of Cassius when facing defeat in the battle of Philippi.

Fear can cause a person to run from a battle they might have won. The Philippian saints are facing a group of people hostile to the Word of God and the ministry of Paul. But for the sake of the gospel, they are to be steadfast in their faith toward those who are entrenched against them.

. . . which (failure on your part to be frightened) is to them an evident token (*endeixis*: proof) of perdition (*apoleia*: their utter destruction), but to you of salvation, and that of (from) God.

God gives us outward symbols of spiritual truths in our lives. These symbols show the world what God has done for us. The lack of fear in the life of the Philippian saints is an outward token or badge of salvation. It shows those in opposition to the gospel that they do not have what the believer has.

The believer knows he has received eternal life, and his lack of fear is an outward display of this. To the one rejecting eternal life, this supernatural lack of fear is also a symbol of his own coming destruction. Through it, he sees the believer's eternal life and his own eternal damnation.

1:29 For to you it has been granted on behalf of Christ, not only to believe in Him, but also to suffer for His sake,

Since we live on this earth as ambassadors and representatives of Jesus Christ, we will suffer the same as He did (Matthew 10:24–25). We are called to believe on the Lord and stand for Him during the hardships of life. How we stand for Him during pressures will be an outward testimony of our faith (James 2:20, 26). Our witness is not only our words but our actions and deeds as well (Colossians 3:17). We are filled with the Holy Spirit not to do witnessing but to be a witness.

1:30 having the same conflict which you saw in me and now hear is in me.

The Philippian saints had already seen how Paul had suffered for the gospel and were hearing of his present opposition. Those who opposed Paul would not accept the Lord Jesus as Savior. They were entrenched against him as many in Philippi were toward the believers there. Just as Paul's badge of eternal life (his lack of fear) made his adversaries angry, so the Philippians' lack of fear would anger their own adversaries.

Chapter Summary

The Lord Jesus suffered. In 1 Corinthians 11:1, Paul writes, "Be ye followers of me, even as I also (am) of Christ." If Paul was truly following the Lord and suffered, then we who follow the Lord — and Paul — will suffer also.

If we, like Paul, will allow the grace of God to operate in and through us during times of suffering, we will see God's plan come to pass, and Christ will be magnified in our lives. Our response to that suffering will be a strong witness to those around us.

2:1–30 The Joy of Sharing the Lord's Humility in Service

The Challenge of Chapter Two

In chapter 1, Paul's admonition to the Philippians concerned how to respond to their enemies. In this chapter, the issue will be how to respond to their brothers and sisters in the body of Christ.

In chapter 1, we saw that believers will never experience unity with the world. Our object is not to live in harmony with those who reject God, but rather, to win them over to the Lord Jesus Christ. On the other hand, we are to live in harmony and peace with those in the body of Christ. The same Holy Spirit who gives us power to witness to the world also enables us to live in unity with each other.

Unity is difficult for the world to attain. Through legislation — and sometimes intimidation — governments try to get people of different races, cultures, and backgrounds to live in harmony with each other with varying success.

The church is also filled with people from different races, cultures, and backgrounds. We are to be an example to the world of the power of the new birth, the Word of God, and the Holy Spirit. What the world cannot do, the supernatural power of God can.

A sad thing happens when the church starts to live like the world. Paul heard from prison that factions were developing in the Philippian church. Here He writes to remind them of the Holy Spirit who lives in them and the fruit which He produces.

I. The Fellowship of Love (1–11)

In these verses, Paul sets a standard for unity among believers by showing the example Jesus gave us through His humility and His exaltation.

> 2:1 ¶ Therefore if *there* is any consolation in Christ, if any comfort of love, if any fellowship of the Spirit, if any affection and mercy,

If there be therefore, any consolation (*paraklesis*: encouragement, exhortation) in Christ . . .

In this verse, Paul lists four areas in which the Holy Spirit empowers every believer. These areas are not something we attain, but what we already possess by having received this power at the point of salvation.

The first area is encouragement in Christ. Just as the Lord encourages us, we are to encourage each other. Instead of encouraging divisions and separations, we are to encourage each other toward unity. Our example is the Lord Jesus and the unity of the body of Christ.

. . . if any comfort (*paramuthion*: persuasion) of (from) love . . .

The second area is the persuasion which comes from love. Agape love is the motivating force behind our persuasion toward each other. Not only are we to encourage each other, but the attitude behind it should be for the benefit of the other person, not for ourselves or our own ends.

. . . if any fellowship (*koinonia*: partnership) of the Spirit . . .

The third area is partnership of the Spirit. We do not encourage each other from our own strength but from the power of the Holy Spirit who is in intimate partnership with us. Just as we are partners with the Holy Spirit, we are partners with each other.

. . . if any bowels (*splagchnon*: affections) and mercies (*oiktirmos*: compassions),

The fourth area is affections and compassions. The care we have for each other should come from deep within. This is the true compassion and not a facade or a veneer of caring. Genuine love is "without hypocrisy" (1 Timothy 1:5).

2:2 fulfill my joy by being like-minded, having the same love, *being* of one accord, of one mind.

Fulfill (*pleroo*) ye my joy . . .

At one time, Paul's joy for the Philippians had been running over, but recent reports that they had lost their unity causes him concern. After acknowledging the power of the Holy Spirit available to every believer in the above verses, Paul asks the Philippians to walk in unity and restore his joy.

. . . that ye be likeminded (*phroneo*: think the same thoughts), having the same love (*agape*), being of one accord (*sumpsuchos*: joined in soul) . . .

At one time, the congregation at Philippi had a singleness of purpose: they loved Paul and his message so much that, out of their joy for the Lord, they gave to his need and the work of the ministry. When a church becomes single-minded, joined in soul, they seek the well being of each other, not their own. They focus on the goal of the Christian life which is winning souls and seeing to it each life is supplied with answers for daily problems.

Just as Paul's joy could be made complete by the Philippians' obedience to the Word, their joy could be made complete by each other's response to the will of God. A person will have their joy complete when their needs are met and they are actively helping meet the needs of others.

. . . of one mind (*phroneo*: thinking one thing, occupied with one vision).

Not only are the Philippians to think the same thoughts, they are to keep a common vision within the church (3:14–15). This keeps divisions and factions from erupting and prevents splits over doctrinal differences. When a church is united in this way, the minister is filled with joy.

> **2:3 *Let* nothing *be done* through selfish ambition or conceit, but in lowliness of mind let each esteem others better than himself.**

Let nothing be done through strife (*eritheia*: contention, selfishness) or vainglory (*kenodoxia*: empty praise, vanity) . . .

The opposite of unity is division and self-seeking. When good works are done in the church that are not motivated by love but rather strife and contention, it amounts to wood, hay, and stubble.

These conditions exist when people begin to work for the admiration of others. A competition takes over for the attention of those in charge. Hypocrisy takes the place of true love and spirituality. Pride rises up in members of the congregation, and some strive to be the spiritual "king of the mountain." This is legalism.

. . . but in lowliness of mind (*tapeinophrosune*: humility, grace thinking) let each esteem others (one another) better than themselves.

Instead of high-mindedness, the congregation should take on the attitude of seeing each other as better than themselves. Jesus Christ Himself gave us an example. He took the position of a servant and washed the feet of His disciples. These attributes in a church ensure stability, longevity, and a flow of love between the people.

2:4 Let each of you look out not only for his own interests, but also for the interests of others.

I am so glad for the "also" in this verse. Paul has been encouraging us to be unselfish: the "also" gives us a balance to keep us out of the ditch on the other side of the road; from only thinking about others and never ourselves. I have known believers who think so poorly of themselves that they only live their lives for others. False humility is also a stench in God's nostrils (Colossians 2:18, 23). We are to look at both our own things and the things of others.

Keeping this balance in life, we pay tithes to the church and also put food in our family's mouths. We do not neglect our family for the sake of the Lord. We give to others what we can give and do not sacrificially give to the exclusion of other important areas of life.

A. Jesus as Our Example: His Humility

2:5 ¶ Let this mind be in you which was also in Christ Jesus,

Let this mind (*phroneo*: think this–imperative mood) be in you (among yourselves), which was also in Christ Jesus:

The common thinking within the local church should be to have the mind of Christ. If the goal of the people is to think like the Lord, no division can occur. Striving for the same goal and vision (3:13–14) as well as thinking on the Word of God ensures success, stability, and longevity for the congregation.

2:6 who, being in the form of God, did not consider it robbery to be equal with God,

Who, being (*huparcho*: existing) in the form (*morphe*: outward display) of God . . .

In eternity past, as deity, Christ was always equal with the Father in His essence. All three members of the Godhead are coequal and coeternal. They do not each possess a third of the love, power, and knowledge. Rather, all three possess the same full measure of these divine attributes.

. . . thought it not robbery (*harpagmos*: a thing to be grasped at) to be equal (*isos*: exactly equal) with God:

Christ did not possess a false humility and have to struggle or grasp for the realization that He was equal with God. It was not a difficult thought for Him. Being altogether sure of His position as deity, He did not have any trouble coming down to man's level and redeeming him.

2:7 but made Himself of no reputation, taking the form of a bondservant, *and* coming in the likeness of men.

But made himself of no reputation (*kenoo*: emptied himself) and took upon him the form (*morphe*: appearance) of a servant, and was made (*ginomai*: became made) in the likeness (*homoioma*: resemblance) of men (*anthropos*: mankind):

Jesus did not empty Himself of His deity, but the glory and reputation of it. He did not come into this earth displaying His deity, but His humanity. He let His words, teaching, and lifestyle display His deity. Neither did He come into this earth to show His authority, but His willingness to submit to the will of the Father and to meet the needs of men. Jesus came into this earth as a man to redeem mankind.

This same mindset is to be in us. We, too, can know we are equal with God in light of the new birth and its provisions, yet take on the form of a servant to meet the needs of others and bring them into the plan of God. The mission of the Lord Jesus on the earth becomes our mission. Just as Jesus was an ambassador for the Father, we too become ambassadors to do the will of God (2 Corinthians 5:20).

This thinking is to control our individual and corporate lives in the Church. Following Christ's example, we are to give our lives daily for those around us, that we may bring them to heaven with us.

B. Jesus as Our Example: His Suffering

2:8 And being found in appearance as a man, He humbled Himself and became obedient to *the point of* death, even the death of the cross.

And being found (*heurisko*: having been recognized) in fashion (*schema*: by outward appearance) as a man . . .

Jesus lowered Himself to the level of man when He was born into the earth (Hebrews 2:9). He was easily recognized as a man by those He met. Yet even though he was a man, he was not a fallen man. He was God manifested in the flesh (John 1:14). He was a perfect man. Because of the virgin birth, He was born without the sinful nature of the flesh.

. . . he humbled (*tapeinoo*: made low) himself, and became obedient (*hupekoos*) unto death, even the death of the cross.

The reason Jesus had to become a man was to die for the sins of the world. The penalty for sin is death (Romans 6:23), but, as deity, He could not die. He had to become man to be subject to death. It was one step down to submit to become man; it was another step down to submit to death, especially on the cross.

Jesus entered this world under submission to the law of Moses (Luke 2:2, Galatians 4:4) which demanded a perfect life (freedom from the sin nature) and then death of the sinless substitute (Leviticus 1:3). His natural life was submission to an existence as a carpenter's son. He was betrayed for the price of a bond slave (Exodus 21:32). He then humbled Himself to die on the cross, a method of execution reserved for criminals from the lowest level of society. These are the types of people Jesus identified with in His death so they could be exalted into the throne room of God and be seated with God the Father as He Himself was.

C. Jesus as Our Example: His Exaltation

2:9 Therefore God also has highly exalted Him and given Him the name which is above every name,

Wherefore (because of this) God (the Father) also hath highly exalted (*huperupsoo*: lifted above and beyond) him . . .

Because of his self-humiliation, the Father (and Holy Spirit, Romans 8:11) brought Jesus back from the dead and seated Him back in heaven at the right hand of God the Father. He was then given a unique title as Head of All Angels (Hebrews 1:4) and Head of the Church (Ephesians 1:19–23). As the resurrected Christ, He received a position and status which He never had when He was Deity only. As the God-man, He is also our great high priest (Hebrews 2:17). His exaltation opened the way for us to enter His presence in human form.

. . . and given (*charizomai*: given out of grace) him a name which is above every name:

The name given the resurrected Christ is not the title of deity, which is always a superior name. Rather, it is the name of His humanity. In His humanity, he conquered the works of Satan, rose from the dead, and sat at the right hand of glory (Hebrews 1:3). And so we pray and stand in faith in the name of our Lord's humanity, "Jesus" (Acts 3:6, 16).

> **2:10 that at the name of Jesus every knee should bow, of those in heaven, and of those on earth, and of those under the earth,**

That (with a result that) at the name of Jesus every knee should bow (*kampto*: bend) . . .

Bowing of the knee represents the attitude of the heart, the place where we believe (Romans 10:9–10).

This verse emphasizes the doctrine of unlimited atonement. Jesus died so everyone could be saved; however, our salvation is dependent on our submission to Him. This is our knee bending, and he died to give everyone the same opportunity.

. . . of things in heaven (*epouranios*: the heavens), . . .

These are high-ranking demons which rule countries, kingdoms, and nations (Ephesians 6:12). Although these creatures know the lordship of Jesus Christ, there is no salvation for them.

. . . and things in earth (*epigeios*: upon the earth), . . .

This includes all people of every nation and country. Those who believe on the Lord will be saved. Jesus died to settle the angelic conflict and bring man to the point of decision.

. . . and things under the earth (*katachthonios*: beneath the earth);

This includes the entire satanic kingdom including fallen angels bound in hell (Tartarus) (2 Peter 2:4, Jude 6).

> **2:11 and *that* every tongue should confess that Jesus Christ is Lord, to the glory of God the Father.**

And that every tongue (*glossa*) should confess (*exomologeo*: admit openly, acclaim) that Jesus Christ is Lord (Acts 16:31, Romans 10:9–10).

The outward confession is a result of inwardly believing on the Lord. The verb tense of both the actions of confessing and knee bowing in verse 10 shows these remain potential until the day of the second advent. On that day, as the world sees Jesus return to establish His kingdom, everyone will be confessing His lordship. However, for all those on the earth, it will be too late.

. . . to the glory (*eis doxa*: for the glory) of God the Father.

When a person believes in his heart and confesses with his mouth that Jesus is Lord, God the Father, who originated the plan of redemption, is glorified. Everyone who believes confirms the defeat of Satan, proving that God was right for throwing him out of heaven.

After we receive Jesus, our daily walk of faith gives glory to God because we produce God's will in the devil's world. This proves Satan is not omnipotent. He has no control over a person's will. (God can coerce man's will but doesnot. Satan cannot coerce man's will but would if he could). The people of the world are free to choose for or against the Lord.

II. The Essentials of Christian Service (12–16)

These verses exhort us to demonstrate our own salvation through Christian service. Paul details the essential actions and heart attitudes God requires.

A. Exhortation to Work Out Our Own Salvation

> **2:12 ¶ Therefore, my beloved, as you have always obeyed, not as in my presence only, but now much more in my absence, work out your own salvation with fear and trembling;**

Wherefore (*hoste*: so then, consequently) my beloved . . .

This is a result clause. Based on the Lord's obedience and delivery of salvation to us, we are to take that new birth and begin to produce our new nature in our daily lives.

. . . as ye have always (*pantote*: at all times) obeyed (*hupakouo*: to obey by listening) . . .

The meaning of this phrase in the Greek is "to answer the door." Whenever the Philippians have heard the Word of God, they have opened the door of obedience. Paul now asks them to further obey as they always have and move into new areas of discipline and sanctification.

. . . not as in my presence (*parousia*) only, but now much more in my absence (*apousia*), work out (*katergazomai*: something on the inside working itself to the outside) your own salvation . . .

The Philippian believers now need to step further into God's plan and grow up. God placed the salvation inside of them. They need to bring it out. It needs to be manifested in their everyday walk before the world. Notice it's their own salvation they need to be working out, not everyone else's. We cannot live each others' lives. We all have a full-time job running our own lives.

. . . with fear (*phobos*) and trembling (*tromos*).

This indicates an obsession to do it right. Maximum effort should go into our outward life before the world. God does a perfect job in placing the new birth in us. What God does in us has no mistakes; however, our own efforts to express the new birth in actions can be flawed. We need to see our every action as an outward witness to the world.

2:13 for it is God who works in you both to will and to do for *His* good pleasure.

For (*gar*: this is the reason) it is God which worketh (*energeo*: produces) in (inside) you both to will (desire) and to do (produce) of his good pleasure (*eudokia*: satisfaction).

The good pleasure of God is placed in us by the Lord at salvation. The desire to produce that good pleasure and live it before the world also comes from the Lord. There is no good work we can produce which does not spring from a godly desire and is not accomplished by His power.

B. Essential Actions and Attitudes

2:14 ¶ Do all things without complaining and disputing,

Do all things without murmurings (*goggusmos*: grumbling, muttering in a low voice) and disputings (*dialogismos*: criticism, skeptical questionings):

When producing the good works which God has willed to do in us, we are to do it with a right attitude. This means things are done in fellowship and with an attitude of love. When we are in fellowship, we are under the control of the Holy Spirit who sheds love abroad in our hearts. This keeps our lives from being hypocritical.

Our attitude is part of our witness before the world. We are not only to speak our witness and regard each action as a witness, but also to show forth a proper attitude in everything we say and do.

2:15 that you may become blameless and harmless, children of God without fault in the midst of a crooked and perverse generation, among whom you shine as lights in the world,

That (*hina*: in order that) ye may be (*ginomai*) blameless (*amemptos*: without cause for blame) and harmless (*akeraios*: pure, unadulterated) (cf. Ephesians 1:4, 5:27) . . .

All of this is for our continued growth and maturity. God wants us to be stable believers in an unstable world. We show His life to the unbelievers around us as we mature and "work out" our salvation.

. . . the sons (*teknon*: children) of God, without rebuke (*amometos*: spot, blemish, fault) . . .

This verse does not mean the world will not rebuke us, rather that they will have no reason for their criticism. They may even use our spotlessness for an excuse to ridicule us. But it is commendable to the Lord if we suffer for this reason (1 Peter 2:19–20).

. . . in the midst (*mesos*: middle) of a crooked (*skolios*: bent) and perverse (*diastrepho*: twisted, distorted, perverted) nation (generation) . . .

We get the medical term "scoliosis" from this *skolios*.

Our witness before the world should be as obvious as a straight rope placed in the middle of ropes that are twisted into knots. Only the new birth and the Word of God can take an unbeliever whose life is bent by sin and twisted by the world's viewpoint and straighten it out.

The world cannot itself because its problems are not natural, but supernatural. They must be seen through the eyes of the Spirit and understood in light of the conflict between the kingdom of light and the kingdom of darkness. A mature believer is the only one who can properly perceive and understand the world's problems.

. . . among whom (crooked and perverse) ye shine (*phaino*) as lights (*phoster*: great lights) in the world;

The analogy here is of the sun and moon which shine forth their lights in the darkness of outer space. This is how we are in the devil's darkened world. The more maturity we walk in, the more light we give forth (Matthew 5:14). The world's system is filled with corruption because it is backed by Satan, the god of this world (1 John 4:4). This will not be completely changed until the second advent of Jesus Christ. In the meantime, we are ambassadors in His place (2 Corinthians 5:20). He was the original light of God the Father (John 1:7–9, Hebrews 1:3), and now as mature believers, we have been called to shine in His place until His return.

2:16 holding fast the word of life, so that I may rejoice in the day of Christ that I have not run in vain or labored in vain.

Holding forth (*epecho*: holding out) the word (*logos*: message) of life (*zoe*)
. . .

Epecho is the word pictured here of a hand holding out food or drink to a starving and thirsting man.We hold out what the world is really looking for. They may not know or want to admit that their true need is Jesus Christ and eternal life, but we know and expect the Holy Spirit to take our message and bring conviction. When a sinner hears the truth, he knows it. His spirit recognizes that eternal life in Christ is what he has been really looking for.

. . . that I may rejoice (*kauchema*: boast, glory) in the day of Christ . . .

The "day of Christ" is the time of the judgment seat of Christ. We will all stand before this seat (Romans 14:10–11, 2 Corinthians 5:9–10) and give an account of our works before the Lord. At this time, we will be rewarded (1 Corinthians 3:10–15). On this day, Paul wants much to boast about before the Lord. This boasting will come because he made full proof of his ministry and held out eternal life to those in need in the world.

This is the message and ministry we all have in this earth before sinners. This is also the main area we will be rewarded for at the judgment seat of Christ.

. . . that I have not run (*trecho*) in vain (*kenos*: emptily, for naught). . . .

Here Paul makes reference to a runner in an athletic game who runs a race but is disqualified at the end. Paul wants all of his hard work to count for something.

Legalism is what disqualifies us in the Christian race. Paul knows he could be disqualified from receiving the rewards for his life if he allows the law to enter as a means of salvation or spirituality. Our works are not a means of spirituality or salvation but a result of them.

Paul wants his torch to shine brightly and his message to the world of eternal life to not be clouded by human effort or man-made standards.

. . . neither labored (*kopiao*: work hard) in vain.

Works have to enter into the picture, but it is possible for all of our works to be burned up as wood, hay, and stubble before the judgment seat of Christ (1 Corinthians 3:10–15). Paul wants the proper motive behind the works so he can receive the proper reward for them in "the day of Christ."

III. Examples of Humility in Service (17–30)

The third section provides us with examples from the lives of Paul, Timothy, and Epaphroditus.

A. The Example of Paul

2:17 ⁋ Yes, and if I am being poured out *as a drink offering* on the sacrifice and service of your faith, I am glad and rejoice with you all.

Yea, and (*kai*: even) if I be offered (*spendo*: poured out as a drink offering) upon (on top of) the sacrifice (*thusia*) . . .

This drink offering was poured out on the ground in front of the heathen deities (Romans 15:16, 2 Timothy 4:6). Paul realizes he may not get to live his life out and stand before the Lord with a completed race. He may have to die first as a martyr (1:20–23).

. . . and (even) service (*leitourgia*: sacred service) of your faith (*pistis*), I joy, and rejoice with you all.

The sacrifice Paul made to the Lord was in spiritual service to the faith of the Philippians.

Paul is saying here that he might have his lifeblood poured out as wine on the ground, but if this is the Lord's will, he will accept it. Even if his life only added a small fragrance to the offering and service of the Philippians, he rejoiced that he had a part to play in their spiritual advancement.

2:18 For the same reason you also be glad and rejoice with me.

For the same cause (in like manner) also do ye joy (*chairo*: rejoice), and rejoice with (*sugchairo*: share your rejoicing with) me.

If Paul is to be sacrificed and have his lifeblood poured out, he wants the Philippians to rejoice on their own and also rejoice with him.

Death for any believer brings sorrow to those who remain, but it also brings rejoicing for even the smallest part they shared with our lives. Paul is saying that even if his life had only offered a small portion of help to the Philippians, he would want to rejoice and share their rejoicing with him at his death.

B. The Example of Timothy

2:19 ¶ But I trust in the Lord Jesus to send Timothy to you shortly, that I also may be encouraged when I know your state.

But I trust (*elpizo*: hope) in the Lord Jesus to send Timotheus shortly unto you, that I also may be (*ginomai*) of good comfort (*eupsuche*), when (after) I know your state.

Here, Paul declares his trust in the Lord that he would not die and would be able to send Timothy to Philippi before his release from prison. His plan is for Timothy to bring back news of the Philippians so he can be comforted by the good report. Paul had joy in prison when he thought of the Philippians but would have great comfort when he heard Timothy's first-hand report of their condition.

2:20 For I have no one like-minded, who will sincerely care for your state.

For I have no man likeminded (*isopsuchos*: of equal soul, confidence) who will naturally (*gnesios*: genuinely) care (*merimnao*: be concerned) for your state (circumstances).

There were others Paul could send to Philippi, but none had the true love and affection for the people that Timothy had. Timothy had stayed behind in Philippi to lead the church there when Paul and Silas traveled to Thessalonica and Berea. Timothy knew the heart of the people.

Paul was sure the church at Philippi would genuinely receive Timothy, and he would truly receive them. Paul also knew the report Timothy would bring back would be filled with love and truth.

Timothy had the same love and affection for the Philippians as Paul did. They were like-minded or of the same soul. Timothy was like a son to Paul in the ministry. When Timothy went into a situation, he tried to handle it as if Paul were there himself. Paul knew this and put great confidence in him.

2:21 For all seek their own, not the things which are of Christ Jesus.

For all (*hoi pontes*: one and all) seek their own (things), not the things which are Jesus Christ's (of Christ Jesus).

Timothy was an exception to the rule among ministers. Not many ministers would serve another and seek only the interests of the Lord Jesus. Most were seeking their own promotion and trying to establish their own ministry. Everything they did had an ulterior motive and was designed to promote themselves.

When these men made decisions, they were not necessarily the best for the church or the minister they worked for. They made decisions to make themselves look good for the next position they planned on moving into. Each day was one step closer to the "ultimate" ministry they hoped to maintain.

These ministers are putting their trust more in their own qualifications than in being faithful where God has placed them. They have forgotten the reality of God's ability to promote. If God does not promote, there is no real promotion.

2:22 But you know his proven character, that as a son with *his* father he served with me in the gospel.

But ye know (*ginosko*: know from experience) the proof (*dokime*: approval of character after being tested) of him, that, as a son (*teknon*: child) with the father, he hath served (*douleuo*: served as a slave) with me in (the spreading of) the gospel.

One reason Timothy had Paul's mind and soul was because of the many years he traveled with him (2 Timothy 2:2). Paul had many good men who were trained under him but none who better understood his heart and passion for the gospel. For example, Titus was a troubleshooter sent into many areas to begin works and pull existing churches into shape.

Yet despite his great ministerial abilities, he did not have the pastor's heart of Paul or Timothy.

Paul said Timothy was "like a son" to him. When Paul left the church at Philippi, he did not leave them in the hands of just anyone. Paul chose Timothy to stay with them because he knew and trusted him.

Paul shows here the most important part of a minister's life is the relationship he has with those around him rather than the knowledge or qualifications he possesses. The reason why Paul recommends Timothy to the Philippians is the relationship the two had and not Timothy's popularity or the number of sermons he knew.

2:23 Therefore I hope to send him at once, as soon as I see how it goes with me.

Him therefore I hope to send presently (*exautes*: at once, immediately), so soon as (*hotan*: whenever) I shall see (*apeido*: turn my attention toward) how it will go with me.

Paul lets the Philippians know he plans to send Timothy but also indicates the uncertainty of the situation. Up until now, Paul has been preoccupied with his own situation in Rome, the conditions with the churches there, and the advancement of the gospel inside and out of prison.

2:24 But I trust in the Lord that I myself shall also come shortly.

But I trust (*peitho*: have come to the settled conclusion or conviction) in the Lord that I also myself shall come shortly.

As Paul turns his attention away from the prison situation and concentrates on the Philippians and their problems, he becomes convinced that he himself will soon be able to visit them as well. (Whether or not Paul ever made this visit has never been proven by historical evidence).

C. The Example of Epaphroditus

2:25 ¶ Yet I considered it necessary to send to you Epaphroditus, my brother, fellow worker, and fellow soldier, but your messenger and the one who ministered to my need;

Yet I supposed it necessary (*anagkaios*: compelling) to send to you Epaphroditus, my brother, and companion in labour (*sunergos*: fellow worker), and fellow soldier (*sustratiotes*). . .

Paul considers Epaphroditus very important to the ministry and gives him one of the highest compliments as a member of his team by calling him "fellow worker" and "fellow soldier." These two stood side by side during Paul's toughest assignments and hardships. Together they weathered the attacks of religious leaders and saw difficult churches established in many Gentile cities.

. . . but your messenger (*apostolos*: representative, ambassador, one to whom you entrusted a mission), and he that ministered (*leitourgos*: ministered in a sacred way) to my wants (*chreia*: needs).

An apostle is not only one who establishes churches, but also one who is sent on a mission either by an individual or by a group of people.

To Paul, Epaphroditus is a fellow soldier, but to the Philippians, he was their apostle. He was sent by the Philippians to take an offering to Paul and to report of the condition of the church at Philippi. This good report refreshed Paul greatly while he was in prison (4:18).

Here Paul assures the Philippian believers that Epaphroditus ministered to his needs. Like Timothy, Epaphroditus did not think of himself only but also saw to the needs of Paul when they were traveling and working together.

2:26 since he was longing for you all, and was distressed because you had heard that he was sick.

For (*epeide*: since then) he longed (*epipotheo*: yearned) after you all, and was full of heaviness (*ademoneo*), because that ye had heard that he had been sick (*astheneo*: distressed, half distracted).

Epaphroditus was moved greatly when he heard the Philippians were concerned about his sickness. When he heard about the love poured out toward him from the saints at Philippi, he wanted very much to come and see them. He was filled with heaviness because of their separation, and he became half distracted in the ministry with Paul because he so desired to be with them.

He wanted to see them, to thank them for praying for him, and to minister to them, teaching them from the Word of God. This would witness to them the healing power of God which had ministered to him and healed him from his sickness.

2:27 For indeed he was sick almost unto death; but God had mercy on him, and not only on him but on me also, lest I should have sorrow upon sorrow.

For indeed (*kai gar*: for even) he was sick nigh unto (*paraplesion*: near to) death: but God had mercy (*eleeo*: showed mercy) on him; and not on him only, but on me also, lest I should have (*echo*) sorrow (*lupe*) upon sorrow.

Paul lets the Philippians know how sick Epaphroditus really was. He was almost dead before the Lord healed him and raised him back to health. This was done not only for his own sake but also for Paul's. God did not want to see sorrow added to sorrow in Paul's life. Being in prison was hardship enough without having Epaphroditus die also.

We are not told why Epaphroditus was sick, but it may have been his own fault. He may have worked too hard or even desired to go on to be with the Lord. However, God intervened and raised him up to continue to minister beside Paul.

2:28 Therefore I sent him the more eagerly, that when you see him again you may rejoice, and I may be less sorrowful.

I sent him therefore the more carefully (*spoudaioteros*: with urgency), that, when ye see him again, (again) ye may rejoice, and that I may be the less sorrowful (*alupos*: without grief).

Paul sent Epaphroditus with urgency to the Philippians so they could rejoice again and Paul would be relieved to know they were no longer concerned for his health.

2:29 Receive him therefore in the Lord with all gladness, and hold such men in esteem;

Receive (*prosdechomai*: welcome) him therefore in the Lord with all gladness (*chara*: joy); and hold such (a one) in reputation (*entimos*: honor):

The Philippians were to receive Epaphroditus in joy and uphold him as an esteemed member of not only the ministry, but also of the body of Christ.

2:30 because for the work of Christ he came close to death, not regarding his life, to supply what was lacking in your service toward me.

Because of the work of Christ he was nigh (*eggizo*: came near) unto death, not regarding (*parabouleuomai*: having gambled, exposed) his life, to supply your lack (*anapleroo*: filled up your deficiency) of service (*leitourgia*: ministry) toward me.

The word *parabouleuomai* was used of a fighter going into the ring and gambling with his own life. This is what Epaphroditus had done. He was putting so much effort into the ministry, he had not taken care of his body. He had reached the point of burning out for the Lord's work. Fortunately, God had compassion on his lack of wisdom and healed him.

Epaphroditus had not paid attention to Paul's sermon to the Ephesian pastors to "take heed to yourselves and to all the flock" (Acts 20:28). No minister is to run himself into the ground and work so hard he ends up dying early. This is not the will of God.

Chapter Summary

Jesus was a servant. He gave us an amazing lesson in humility when He stepped down from His high rank as deity to serve and to lay down His life for mankind.

His life establishes the pattern for God's promotion. Humble yourself to obey the will of God, being willing, if necessary, to suffer for righteousness sake and God will exalt you: "Humble yourselves therefore under the mighty hand of God, that he may exalt you in due time" (1 Peter 5:6).

When we are born again, we receive a new nature with the ability to love and serve like the Lord Jesus.

However, it is left up to each of us, individually, to bring out that salvation and to show it before the world. If we truly follow Christ's example, we will serve others without grumbling or criticism, motivated by love.

If we joyfully share the Lord's humility in service, gladly giving our lives daily for those around us, we are sure to bring many to heaven with us and to receive our full reward.

3:1–21 The Joy of Maturing in Christ

The Challenge of Chapter Three

As we grow in the Lord and become familiar with the dos and don'ts of the Christian life, it is easy to get complacent. We reason, "I know what the Scripture says, so why continue to study it?" We go through the outward motions of church attendance and Christian service, often becoming overly busy with religious activities. We think we have arrived.

Paul, in this stunning chapter, challenges us to "put no confidence" in accomplishments, reputation, and knowledge. He states emphatically that all these are totally worthless compared to knowing Christ.

His advice to those who want to continue to grow is to keep doing what they did to get them that far: study the Word and immerse themselves in the thoughts of God. This is God's plan for seizing, possessing, and maintaining maturity.

I. The Priorities of Maturity (1–8)

In these verses, Paul shows the difference between the outward things that religious man counts as important and "gaining Christ," the top priority of true maturity.

3:1 ¶ Finally, my brethren, rejoice in the Lord. For me to write the same things to you is not tedious, but for you *it is* safe.

Finally (*loipon*: a change of subject), my brethren . . .

At the end of the previous chapter, Paul gave examples of Christian service from the lives of three great communicators of the Word of God: Paul, Timothy, and Epaphroditus. He now changes the subject, shifting his attention back to instructing the Philippian believers. Just as Timothy and Epaphroditus learned from Paul's experiences and applied his teachings to their own lives, so the saints in Philippi can also profit from Paul's doctrines.

A. Rejoice in the Lord

. . . rejoice (*chairo*: a supernatural joy and happiness which comes from the Holy Spirit) in the Lord . . .

This joy is reserved for the believer who applies the Word of God to the experiences and trials of life. Faith releases this type of joy in our lives. We can experience a supernatural calm in the middle of a storm because we know our security in Jesus Christ. When a person has an unshakable knowledge that he cannot be destroyed, he can endure any trial or affliction.

Since we are in the Lord, we know we have ultimate security. Even if we never applied one single promise from God's Word to our lives, we would still end up in heaven. If we were killed in persecution, it would not be God's best, but we would still end up winners for eternity.

God's best is for us to rejoice "in the Lord" because we know God has not only provided for eternity but also for this life. He has given promises which are "exceeding great and precious" (2 Peter 1:4). These promises all have power to deliver us from the persecutions and trials brought by Satan and his world system (2 Corinthians 4:4) and, at the same time, produce supernatural happiness through them (John 17:13).

Rejoicing is the outward expression of this inward joy. The calm on the inside overflows to the outside and causes praise and rejoicing "in the Lord."

. . . To write (be writing) the same things to you, to me indeed is not grievous (*okneros*: troublesome, irksome) . . .

Repetitious teaching is not troublesome for a minister who is truly interested in his congregation's growth. Repetition is necessary for people to learn. A pastor who does not repeat his teaching is negligent in his calling (2 Peter 1:12).

. . . but (on the other hand) for you it is safe (*asphales*: safeguard, security).

Security comes to a group of people in a congregation when the pastor teaches by repetition. The important subjects of the Word of God need to be taught many times over for the people to really hear, understand, and remember them. This builds up a foundation in their life which cannot be taken away or torn down through the circumstances and trials of life. For the congregation to reach the point of maturity and for them to be spiritually self-sustaining, they must hear the Word of God again and again.

B. Watch Out for Legalism (and Dogs)

3:2 ¶ Beware of dogs, beware of evil workers, beware of the mutilation!

Beware (*blepo*: look out for) of dogs (*kuon*) . . .

1. In the Word of God, when the label "dog" is applied to people, it is used in a deriding and insulting way.

   a) Of David before Goliath (1 Samuel 17:43).

   b) Of David before Saul (1 Samuel 24:14).

   c) Of Mephibosheth before David (2 Samuel 9:8).

   d) Of the king before Elisha (2 Kings 8:13).

2. The most dishonorable death of the Old Testament was to be devoured by dogs (1 Kings 14:11, 16:4, 21:19, 21:23).

3. "Dog" is used in analogy to reversion (or regression) in the Christian life (Philippians 3:2).

4. "Dog" is often used by Jews to describe Gentiles (Matthew 7:4).

5. "Dog" is used to describe unbelievers (2 Peter 2:22).

6. Criminals and those who live by violence are described as dogs (Psalms 59:6, 14).

7. King Saul's greatest general was a seducer of women and was described as a dog (2 Samuel 3:8).

8. Dogs were used to administrate the destruction of Jerusalem (Jeremiah 15:3).

9. Jesus used the term "dog" to describe someone unworthy to receive blessings (Matthew 15:25–27, Mark 7:25–28).

In the ancient world, dogs were scavengers who carried diseases. Like the coyotes and wolves of today, they roamed in packs and were dangerous to humans. They could not only harm but kill if cornered and were hated and feared by people in the cities.

Paul uses the label "dogs" by analogy to warn the Philippians about spiritual dangers. Paul compared these false teachers to the dogs of his day: scavengers who came from outside, traveled in packs, and could prove deadly.

Although the Jews often used this term to describe Gentiles, Paul now uses it to describe false Jewish teachers, scavengers of the local churches Paul has helped establish. They constantly tried to bring legalism where Paul had taught grace. These men presented themselves as spiritual teachers knowing the deeper things of God, but Paul now exposes them in this verse for what they truly are.

. . . beware (*blepo*) of evil (*kakos*) workers (*ergates*: workmen) . . .

These are the same men Paul referred to as dogs, but now he addresses their production of "human good." They come in with works disguised as divine good. They seem sincere and convincing, but they are dogs nonetheless.

The main opposition to the gospel is always "human good," which is legalism.

. . . beware of the concision (*katatome*: circumcision).

This reference to circumcision is the "evil work" Paul just mentioned. The Jewish teachers would follow Paul and add to the message of grace by saying that circumcision had to be added to faith to truly bring salvation. Others claimed circumcision increased spirituality. This distorted the simplicity of the plan of God and caused great confusion in many of the churches Paul started.

C. Put No Confidence in the Flesh

3:3 For we are the circumcision, who worship God in the Spirit, rejoice in Christ Jesus, and have no confidence in the flesh,

For we are (*eimi*: keep on being) the circumcision . . .

This is an explanation of the previous phrase "beware of the concision." Those who have accepted the Lord as Savior are the circumcision. What is done to our bodies may help us in the physical or natural realms, but will not help us spiritually. God sees us as already spiritually circumcised in the heart (Romans 2:28–29, Colossians 2:11).

"Circumcision" in the New Testament is a type of the law and includes those who live by the law in an attempt to please the Lord (Romans 2:5). Anyone who has added works to the plan of salvation or spirituality is part of the "concision."

. . . which worship (*latreuo*: offer spiritual service) God in the spirit . . .

In the Greek, this literally says, ". . . who worship by the Spirit of God." This is the function of our priesthood in the world. We offer spiritual service to the Lord through the power of the Holy Spirit.

In the Old Testament, the Jewish nation was considered to be the nation of circumcision, the ones chosen to offer up the sacrifices and spiritual service to the Lord.

Now, in the New Testament, the Church stands in that place, worshiping God in spirit and in truth (John 4:24). God has chosen the Church as a new nation, a new people (1 Peter 2:9–10) until the coming of the Lord Jesus.

. . . and rejoice (*kauchaomai*: boast, glory) in Christ Jesus . . .

Our bragging is never in ourselves, or about what we have done, but in the Lord Jesus and what He has done in and for us.

. . . and have no confidence (*peitho*: trust) in the flesh.

As we turn toward something, we also turn away from the flesh. We know the flesh is still unredeemed and is no more capable of pleasing the Lord after salvation than it was before. Since the Lord has no confidence in our flesh, neither should we.

1. Paul's Confidence in the Flesh

Paul has much to say about confidence in the flesh. His self-confidence, plus a strong desire to go to Jerusalem and preach to the Jews, took him on a five-year detour out of the geographic will of God. He was still recovering from that detour when he wrote this epistle.

Paul was headed in the right direction at the writing of Romans because he mentioned to the saints that he would visit them on his way to Spain (Romans 15:24). He decided to take a side trip to Jerusalem (Romans 15:25), and this took him out of the will of God for five years.

During the revival at Ephesus — when a riot broke out started by the silversmith union under Demetrius (Acts 19:23–41) — Paul was shaken up in the riot and called his disciples together to inform them he was headed toward Macedonia (Acts 20:1). He was still in compliance with his orders until he came to Corinth, where he turned and headed for Troas and Jerusalem.

From that time on, he would not turn back, though many prophecies came to him warning him of his wrong decision. In Acts 20:16–38, he was hurrying toward Jerusalem to be there for the feast of Pentecost. Not taking the time to stop in Ephesus, he asked the Ephesian pastors to meet him in

Miletus. There he told them that he would go to Jerusalem to preach and might never see their faces again.

Although Paul was warned again and again not to go to Jerusalem (Acts 21:4–9 and 21:10–13), he completely disobeyed the Holy Spirit and began of a long period of carnality.

2. Paul's Sin of Legalism

By the time Paul arrived in Jerusalem (Acts 21:14–17), he was in full apostasy. He could not think in accordance with grace anymore and took heed of bad advice from the leaders in Jerusalem to walk orderly and keep the law (21:20–24). The champion of grace took a legalistic vow in front of the people (Acts 21:26). He compromised the grace of God in hopes that, by doing so, he could teach the Word to the citizens of Jerusalem.

But one week later, Paul went to the temple to complete his vow and was seen by the legalistic Jews who had stoned him in Lystra. A riot broke out to kill him (Acts 21:27–31). Paul was saved by Roman soldiers who took him into the Mark Antony barracks away from the rioting mob in the streets.

It was apparent that Paul could not leave the barracks and return to the streets because a band of forty Jews had vowed not to eat until Paul was dead (Acts 23:12). Roman command sent Paul, under escort, to the prison in Caesarea, where he was imprisoned at Caesarea for two years during which time he recovered from carnality and apostasy.

Paul stood before Felix (Acts 24), Festus (Acts 25), and Agrippa (Acts 26), three of the most famous judges of Rome. Festus, desiring to do the Jews a favor, wanted to try Paul in Jerusalem, but Paul knew he would not receive a fair trial there and appealed to Caesar in Rome.

He was sent to Rome by ship, a journey which took one year. On the way, he was shipwrecked on Malta. He finally ended up in Rome where he was put under house arrest for two years. While imprisoned, he wrote epistles to the Ephesians, the Philippians, the Colossians, and Philemon.

Through this ordeal, Paul matured to the point that he no longer puts confidence in his own abilities or knowledge, but in Christ.

3:4 though I also might have confidence in the flesh. If anyone else thinks he may have confidence in the flesh, I more so:

Though (even though) I might also have confidence in the flesh. . . .

As far as natural confidence, Paul could have stood head and shoulders over those who came against him all through his life. Paul had confidence now as a believer, but it was in the Lord and His might (Ephesians 6:10). Confidence in a person's own power, personality, and education is arrogance. God cannot stand arrogance (Proverbs 3:34, James 4:6, 1 Peter 5:5) and resists that type of person.

. . . If any man thinketh (*dokeo*: assumes) that he hath whereof he might trust (put confidence) in the flesh, I more;

This is a reference to the false Jewish teachers and prophets. They think they have a lot to brag about, but have not stopped to consider Paul and his background. Paul was a top "celebrity" in his field during the time he was a Pharisee.

3:5 circumcised the eighth day, of the stock of Israel, *of* the tribe of Benjamin, a Hebrew of the Hebrews; concerning the law, a Pharisee;

Circumcised the eighth day, of the stock (*genos*: nationality) of Israel, . . .

Although the Philippians were Gentiles, many had been circumcised after coming to the Lord. Some did this for spiritual reasons, supposing that following after Jewish customs would make them more spiritual. Paul lets them know that if they follow after laws, rules, and regulations for spirituality, someone can always out perform them.

Paul was not circumcised, as many of the Philippians were, late in life, but on the eighth day, as Scripture prescribes. Paul was not a Gentile who received circumcision, but a natural-born Jew.

Paul's statement about circumcision would also be impressive to the Jews, as circumcision was the first issue they pushed when it came to keeping the law for salvation or spirituality.

. . . of the tribe of Benjamin. . .

The tribe of Benjamin was the warrior tribe. This was the tribe who put the first king, Saul, on the throne of Israel. They were loyal to David during the revolution. They were part of the southern kingdom and were a very stable tribe.

. . . an Hebrew of (from) the Hebrews; . . .

This is a reference to Jewish nationalism and patriotism. Paul was from the conservative Hebrew culture as opposed to the liberal Hellenistic culture.

. . . as touching (*kata*: concerning) the law, a Pharisee;

This was Paul's religious background. To be from the tribe of Benjamin was a great thing in the nation of Israel. To be a religious Pharisee was icing on the cake. The Pharisees were the most noted of the religious crowd in Israel. It took much study and diligence to be a member of the Pharisees.

3:6 concerning zeal, persecuting the church; concerning the righteousness which is in the law, blameless.

Concerning (*kata*) zeal, persecuting the church . . .

Of all the persecutors the early church had faced, Paul was the greatest. Interestingly, after Paul's conversion, he was not persecuted by his former comrades, the Jews who had once helped him kill and imprison believers. Rather, he was being persecuted by a different group; men who could not hold a candle to him. When it came to the ability to persecute, these "dogs" were in a different league altogether.

. . . touching (*kata*: concerning) the righteousness (self-righteousness) which is in the law, blameless (*amemptos*).

Paul was a much better law keeper than all of the men who are after him. When it came to the ability to brag in the natural, Paul was far ahead of anyone who came from the nation of Israel. Outward righteousness, the kind which can be seen by all, was far more advanced in Paul's life than anyone else's. At one time, he was a celebrity among the Jews.

3:7 ⚶ But what things were gain to me, these I have counted loss for Christ.

But what things were gain (*kerdos*: advances) to me . . .

Paul's credentials, mentioned in verses 5 and 6, were important to him at one time. Many in the nation of Israel sought all these things. But what the flesh counted as important, Paul now counts as nothing compared to the benefits of the new birth and the spiritual maturity he has found in Jesus

Christ. The Word of God and its application are now the most important things in Paul's life.

. . . those I counted (*hegeomai:* reckoned, concluded) loss (*zemia*) for Christ.

"Gain" in the previous phrase was in the plural. Now "loss" is in the singular. All seven of Paul's credentials were called "gains," but now he calls all of them "one big loss."

3:8 Yet indeed I also count all things loss for the excellence of the knowledge of Christ Jesus my Lord, for whom I have suffered the loss of all things, and count them as rubbish, that I may gain Christ

Yea doubtless (*alla menounge:* most emphatically), and I (therefore I also) count (*hegeomai:* reckon, conclude) all things . . .

"All things" is a reference to anything Paul had before he was saved on the road to Damascus. Anything which came through human achievement or religious zeal will all be counted "loss" and even "dung" by the end of this verse.

. . . but (*eimi:* to be) loss (*zemia*) for the (sake of) excellency (*huperecho:* surpassing greatness) of the knowledge (*gnosis*) of Christ Jesus my Lord . . .

The many areas of Paul's human celebrity status are all in one category, "loss," when compared to the knowledge of Christ found in the Word. As great as all of man's accomplishments are, they are nothing when compared with one revelation found in the Word of God.

. . . for (because of) whom I have suffered the loss of (*zemioo:* forfeited) all things . . .

Paul has made a choice to forfeit all things for the sake of Jesus Christ. He is in no way filled with bitterness or remorse about what he has given up.

. . . and do count (*hegeomai:* conclude) them but dung (*skubalon:* dog castings) . . .

3. Word Study: Dung

a) There are seven words for dung in the Bible: five Hebrew and two Greek. They are used for both the actual waste product and, by analogy, to describe complete worthlessness.

b) The Assyrians threatened Israel with the prospect of eating dung to get them to surrender (2 Kings 18:27, Isaiah 36:12).

c) Dung is used to describe the administration of judgment to a nation when they are defeated by the military of another nation (Zephaniah 1:17). The slain soldiers, left unburied, were seen as dung on the ground (Jeremiah 8:2, 9:22, 16:4, 25:33).

d) Dung is used to describe the judgment of the prosperous wicked (Job 20:4–7).

e) Dung is used to describe the fall of mighty ones (Lamentations 4:5).

f) The interruption of the Jewish age is described as dung on the faces of the priests (Malachi 2:3).

g) Dung is used to describe the uselessness of the apostate believer (Luke 14:34–35).

h) Dung is used to describe human accomplishments and celebrityship (Philippians 3:8).

. . . that (in order that) I may win (*kerdaino*: gain) Christ.

"Gaining Christ" is not a reference to salvation, but to full maturity. This is the same concept found in 1 Timothy 6:12 and 19, "laying hold on eternal life" and 2 Peter 1:4, "be partakers of the divine nature."

II. Maturing Through Grace (9–11)

From the moment of the new birth until we enter eternity, it is the grace of God, not our own righteous deeds, that moves us toward maturity.

A. Grace Orientation at the New Birth

3:9 and be found in Him, not having my own righteousness, which is from the law, but that which *is* through faith in Christ, the righteousness which is from God by faith;

And (also) be found in him . . .

Being "found in Him" occurred at the moment of the new birth. When each of us accepted Jesus as our Savior, we became one with Him and in union with the Godhead. This is part of our positional truth.

. . . not having mine own righteousness (*dikaisoune*) . . .

This righteousness is self-righteousness. It is possible to be "in Christ" and still be self-righteous, controlled by the flesh. This person has no more effect on the world than an unbeliever. He is salt which has lost its savor (Luke 14:34).

. . . which is of (from) the law . . .

The "law" here represents legalism, religion, or human works. These three produce self-righteousness which is always the enemy of the cross and the Christian way of life.

. . . but that (righteousness) which is through (by means of) the faith of (in) Christ . . .

We received righteousness the moment we accepted Jesus as Savior. This is the righteousness we want to be "found in" and showing the world. It is the opposite of self-righteousness. This righteousness is a gift of God which cannot be earned or deserved, neither can we work to keep it.

. . . the righteousness which is of (from the source of) God by (*epi:* based on) faith;

This righteousness did not originate from us but came from God the Father. It is His life, nature, righteousness, and power which we have. We will also share eternity with Him because of His plan, not ours.

B. Grace Orientation in Life

3:10 that I may know Him and the power of His resurrection, and the fellowship of His sufferings, being conformed to His death,

That I may know (*ginosko*) him . . .

The way to "know" God is by taking in His Word consistently. The more we know His Word, the more we know how God thinks. This is truly knowing God. This grace orientation in life leads to maturity and growth in the Lord.

. . . and the power (*dunamis*) of his resurrection . . .

Jesus was raised from the dead by the other two members of the Godhead: the Father (1 Thessalonians 1:10, 1 Peter 1:3) and the Holy Spirit (Romans 8:11, 1 Peter 3:18). The resurrection was the greatest display of power God ever showed (Ephesians 1:19–20, Isaiah 53:1).

The power of the resurrection is made available in our lives as we grow in the Lord. Maturity causes more power to flow through us each day to meet the problems of life. The power of God is brought to us through the daily application of the promises of God (2 Peter 1:3–4).

The potential of daily power offered to us as believers is based on Jesus's resurrection. If it were necessary, God could still give us all the power used to raise up His Son from the dead.

. . . and the fellowship (*koinonia*: participation) of (in) his sufferings (*pathema:* undeserved sufferings), . . .

The more the believer knows the Lord and His Word, the more he is capable of handling the persecutions of life. Paul had reached a place of maturity where his intake of the Word produced so much of the power of God for daily living that he was eager to take on the sufferings of life as Jesus did.

Participation in the sufferings of Jesus has to be preceded with knowing God and His power. Paul was willing to have more persecutions because he knew the unlimited power of God to deliver him was far more than a match for Satan's limited power to cause him suffering. Each trial Paul endured brought glory to God and strength to Paul.

. . . being made conformable (*summorphioo*: taking on the same form) unto his death (*thanatos*);

Paul's sufferings are not the sufferings Jesus took at the cross. Christ's sufferings were unique. They were associated with the penalty for our sins and sicknesses. These came as a result of the fall of Adam and only one, Jesus Christ, the uniquely born Son of God, could suffer these. No one else in history could ever suffer the same way.

The persecutions mentioned here are the sufferings Paul encountered during his lifetime from the religious leaders and from the world, as well as from demons and Satan himself. These sufferings eventually led to his death.

C. Grace Orientation for Eternity

3:11 if, by any means, I may attain to the resurrection from the dead.

If by any means (in some way) I might attain (*katantao*: reach the goal) unto (*eis*) the resurrection (*exanastasis*: out-resurrection) of (from) the dead (*nekros*).

Within the resurrection of the church (the rapture) are ranks or orders (1 Corinthians 15:23). Each rank will be rewarded differently in heaven (1 Corinthians 15:41–42). The rapture is guaranteed to all believers, but ranks within the rapture are determined by the production of divine good during this life. This is not human works under the energy of the flesh, but divine works (*agathos*) produced under the power of the Holy Spirit.

Paul's desire here is not to attain to the resurrection. This was guaranteed him at the new birth (as it is for all believers). Paul's desire is that his reward for knowing God, the power of Christ's resurrection, and the fellowship of his sufferings would be to join the elite group in the resurrection, to shine as the sun, to attain the "out-resurrection."

This goal was not only attainable to Paul then, but is also attainable to each believer in the church today.

III. Maturity in Christ (12–21)

A believer never arrives at perfection; there is always more to be grasped. In these verses, Paul shares how to pursue and maintain deeper levels of maturity.

A. Pursuing Maturity

3:12 ¶ Not that I have already attained, or am already perfected; but I press on, that I may lay hold of that for which Christ Jesus has also laid hold of me.

Not as though I had already attained (*lambano*: received), either were already perfect (*teleioo*) . . .

Paul is not assuming here that he has arrived to the "out-resurrection" or to the full maturity it takes to receive that reward from the Lord. He only knows the goal is out there and that it is attainable. As long as a believer is on earth, God will give him a plan for his life and goals to be attained. Paul still has more advancements to make.

. . . but I follow after (*dioko*: pursue), if that (whether, if) I may apprehend (*katalambano*: seize possession) . . .

The way that all of these goals will be attained in Paul's life — knowing God, the power of His resurrection, the fellowship of His sufferings, and being made conformable to His death — is through constant study of the Word of God. This is God's plan for seizing and possessing the maturity which Paul is pursuing.

. . . that for which (on account of which) also I am apprehended (*katalambano*: seized and overtaken) of (by) Christ Jesus.

The ministry Paul was pursuing and overtaking was the same ministry given to Paul on the road to Damascus when Jesus appeared to him in a blinding light. This ministry seized and held Paul. He could never lose it or the Lord who gave it to him. It is much like salvation and its benefits. We are possessed by salvation, but we also need to possess the benefits of it through spiritual maturity. We all need to overtake that which has overtaken us.

3:13 Brethren, I do not count myself to have apprehended; but one thing I *do*, forgetting those things which are behind and reaching forward to those things which are ahead,

Brethren (saints at Philippi) I count (*logizomai*: estimate, calculate) not myself to have apprehended (*katalambano*: overtaken and gained possession) . . .

Paul has come through the most difficult five years of his life. He headed to Jerusalem out of the will of God and spent two years in Caesarea under Roman protection. He was sent by ship to Rome and ended up in a shipwreck and stranded on Malta. He eventually went to Rome and spent two years there before being released.

Paul now knows he has not "arrived." He used to think he had, and this caused him much trouble. He has now recovered and has learned humility.

As believers, we never arrive. We only continue to get closer to perfection. When we think we have arrived, we become unteachable. This is pride, the direct opposite of meekness. Paul was careless once, but is now watching himself more carefully to ensure it doesn't happen again.

. . . but this one thing I do, forgetting (*epilanthanomai*: assigning to oblivion) those things which are behind . . .

This is the "one thing" Paul does each time the memory comes up of his past mistakes and failures: he assigns them to oblivion. This is something we must do ourselves. It is a mark of maturity to assign a past confessed sin to oblivion instead of pulling it back up and being defeated by an old root of bitterness (Hebrews 12:15).

God assigns our sins to oblivion (1 John 1:9) and a mature believer imitates God (Ephesians 5:1). Even if other people remember your sins, you are commanded to forget them. If they recall your sins to you, do not say "forget those things which are behind." This is not something you can make them do. You can only do it for yourself.

. . . and reaching forth (*epekteinomai*: stretching out) . . .

This comes from taking in the Word of God each day.

. . . unto those things which are before (in front of me),

These are the promises and doctrines of the Word still yet to be learned.

3:14 I press toward the goal for the prize of the upward call of God in Christ Jesus.

I press (pursue) toward the mark (finish line, maturity) for the prize (wreath, crown) of the high (upward) calling of God in Christ Jesus.

There is a place of spiritual maturity which is a high rank in the Lord. Paul is shooting for yet higher ground in maturity. The high calling in life brings him into the "out-resurrection" he mentioned in verse 11. He has failed in grace, but is now coming back. He has his eye on the position of a four-star general, the "high calling."

This position is available to all believers, though few ever attain to it.

B. Living in Maturity

3:15 ¶ Therefore let us, as many as are mature, have this mind; and if in anything you think otherwise, God will reveal even this to you.

Let us (believers) therefore, as many as be perfect (*teleios*), be thus minded . . .

This is an invitation by Paul for us to join him in pressing forward to a higher ground in the Lord. All believers can enjoy this life in maturity, but to attain and maintain it, they have to think like Paul did. They need to forget the mistakes, the failures — and the successes — of the past and continue to look toward what lies ahead.

. . . and if in any thing ye be otherwise minded (think differently), God shall reveal even this unto you.

Many of these people think differently than Paul or their pastor. They may or may not be out of line with the Word of God, but this is not the issue. The issue for the Philippian church or any church today is maturity, the striving together for one common goal. If we together pursue maturity in God's Word, He will reveal to us where our thinking is wrong. This is a major ministry of the Holy Spirit. When our desire is towards the Lord, the Holy Spirit will reveal the Word to us as we pursue spiritual maturity. Many differences which seem major today will be straightened out later and revealed to us by the Holy Spirit.

3:16 Nevertheless, *to the degree* that we have already attained, let us walk by the same rule, let us be of the same mind.

Nevertheless (however) whereto (whatever level) we have attained (advanced to) . . .

Here we have a change of direction. Paul now addresses those believers who have already grown to maturity and are now slacking off. He encourages believers who have attained to any level in the Christian life to keep on and never give up.

. . . let us walk (keep on walking) by the same rule (standard), let us mind the same thing.

When you advance, you must keep doing what caused you to succeed in the first place. The Word of God (and nothing else) has brought these believers to this level of maturity. Now that they have arrived at spiritual maturity, there is no new plan of success outside of the Word.

The congregation as a whole must keep growing by the Word and nothing else. The pastor must be faithful to continue to teach and preach the Word and nothing else.

3:17 ¶ Brethren, join in following my example, and note those who so walk, as you have us for a pattern.

Brethren, be followers (co-imitators) together of me . . .

Paul has come out of his great mistake and has settled back into his pattern of success: taking in the Word daily. He wants the Philippians to do the same thing and not give up.

We know this because, after having achieved and maintained maturity for a number of years, Paul instructs Timothy, who has just recovered from carnality. His advice? Continue in the things which he had learned, scripture given by inspiration of God, which is "profitable for doctrine, for reproof, for correction, for instruction righteousness: that the man of God may be perfect, thoroughly furnished unto all good works" (2 Timothy 3: 16-17)

Each of us will eat natural food for the rest of our lives and not quit. We cannot think we have eaten enough food in thirty or forty years to last the next thirty or forty years! No, we must continue to have a daily intake. The same is true spiritually. We must live by taking in the Word daily (Matthew 4:4).

. . . and mark (*skopeo*: examine, observe) them which walk (keep on walking) so (even so) as ye have us for an example (model).

We all need models in the Christian life (Hebrews 6:12), but not slothful ones who give up after attaining a desired level or goal. We need to look for mature believers and become co-imitators of those who are patient and diligent.

Paul and his team were not the only ones who did not give up. There were many others the Philippians could look to just as there are many today who can serve as role models for us.

C. The Danger of Coasting in the Christian Life

Verses 18 and 19 are parenthetical. Here Paul mentions believers who are not experiencing the joy of maturing in Christ. These people "coast" in the Christian life. Instead of working together for one common goal, they end up in opposition to the Word and at odds with their pastors and other believers in the church.

> **3:18 For many walk, of whom I have told you often, and now tell you even weeping, *that they* are the enemies of the cross of Christ:**

For many walk of whom I have told you often (many times), and now tell you even weeping . . .

Paul has told the Philippians of many who have given up. He has repeatedly told them of those they are not to follow. Paul's heart is broken because of believers he has raised and taught who have left the daily study of God's Word and have quit following the Lord's plan for their lives. The Thessalonians, Galatians, and Corinthians were examples.

. . . that they are (have made themselves) the enemies of the cross of Christ:

The cross begins the plan of God in our lives. Apathy towards the Word pulls us away from the plan and is contrary to the Lord's death, burial, Resurrection, and His present-day seating in the heavenly places.

In the next verse, Paul show us the following results of such apathetic "coasting."

D. Four Results of Giving Up on the Plan of God

1. Sin unto Death

2. Rebellion against God and His Plan

3. Slavery to the Things of This World

4. Blindness to the Divine Viewpoint of Life

3:19 whose end *is* destruction, whose god is *their* belly, and *whose* glory *is* in their shame—who set their mind on earthly things.

Whose end (final outcome) is destruction . . .

The final outcome for someone who rejects the Word of God as a pattern for life is "the sin unto death." A believer can die physically by the hand of Satan. The man in Corinth (1 Corinthians 5:5) and Ananias and Sapphira (Acts 5:1–11) are all examples. The Corinthians who abused communion were also facing the sin unto death (1 Corinthians 11:29–30).

. . . whose God is their belly (*koilia*) . . .

"Belly" or "bowels" are a reference to the person's emotions. These people no longer look at life through the Word of God and the promises of God, but through their emotions and feelings (Romans 16:18, 2 Corinthians 6:11–13).

. . . and whose glory is in their shame (disgrace), who mind earthly things.

Christians who are driven by their emotions, whose feelings become the criteria for life, becomes a slave to the possessions of life. Their values no longer exalt the things of God. They no longer have the divine viewpoint of life but the human, earthly viewpoint as any sinner would.

E. The Divine Viewpoint of Life

3:20 For our citizenship is in heaven, from which we also eagerly wait for the Savior, the Lord Jesus Christ,

For our conversation (*politeuma*: politics, citizenship) is in heaven . . .

Citizenship meant a lot to the people of Philippi. A Philippian citizen was a Roman citizen. They lived in a Roman colony, a city which had all the rights and privileges of the city of Rome.

Paul draws a parallel here to the citizenship of believers. We are citizens of heaven living on earth. We are a heavenly colony just as Philippi was a Roman colony. We enjoy all the rights and privileges of heaven here on earth.

The citizens of Philippi thought and acted as if they live in Rome. The citizens of the royal family of God are to think and act as if they lived in heaven (Colossians 3:1–2). This is part of our ambassadorship (2 Corinthians 5:20).

. . . from whence (heaven) also we look for (anticipate) the Savior, the Lord Jesus Christ,

This is a reference to the rapture of the Church (1 Corinthians 15:51–53, 1 Thessalonians 4:13–17, 2 Thessalonians 2:1–4, 1 John 3:2–3, Colossians 3:4).

> **3:21 who will transform our lowly body that it may be conformed to His glorious body, according to the working by which He is able even to subdue all things to Himself.**

Who (Jesus Christ) shall change (transform) our vile body (body of humiliation), that it may be fashioned (conformed) like unto his glorious body . . .

This is the resurrection body of Jesus Christ. We will have a body just like His. Our body now is weak, fleshly, and corruptible. It will be raised up in power as an incorruptible spiritual body (1 Corinthians 15:42–44).

. . . according to (*kata*) the working (*energeia*: operational power) whereby he is able (*dunamai*) even to subdue all things unto himself.

Until the coming of the Lord Jesus Christ, persecutions will increase from the world and from Satan. Just before the rapture of the church and the time of the tribulation, evil from demonic forces will increase inside and outside the church (Acts 20:29–30).

The same power that will transform our natural bodies into resurrection bodies will subdue everything else on earth at the Lord's Second Advent.

Chapter Summary

Just as there is great joy in salvation, there is also joy in maturing in Christ. Paul has attained this place of joy. It shines through his life and through the words of this epistle.

In this chapter, Paul warns us of three dangers facing those who wish to mature in Christ and win the prize of the high calling.

First, we must forsake legalism in all its forms. The Judaizers missed it. They were zealous for God, yet they never knew the full joy of knowing Jesus and the power of His resurrection. Legalism kills; only the Spirit can give life.

If we are to progress in the Christian life, we must stop measuring ourselves (and others) by external standards to see who is "measuring up" and who isn't.

A second danger is the pitfall of human celebrityship, of living to impress others. Paul, a "Hebrew of the Hebrews," cannot compare to the benefit of knowing Christ.

Third, we must resist the temptation to coast (or rest upon what we have already learned) rather than making sure we continue to feast on the Word of God each day. Only a daily intake of the living Word will give us stability and ensure our spiritual progress.

4:1–23 The Joy of Sharing the Peace of Jesus

The Challenge of Chapter Four

Paul has experienced tremendous suffering caused both by his personal choices and persecution for the gospel's sake. Despite all he has suffered, he has learned to experience a deeply abiding joy and peace, while keeping his heart and mind through Christ Jesus.

I. The Peace of Single-mindedness (1–5)

Paul encourages the Philippians to stand fast in unity, single-mindedness, and moderation, rejoicing always.

> **4:1 Therefore, my beloved and longed-for brethren, my joy and crown, so stand fast in the Lord, beloved.**

Therefore (as a result of the glorious hope), my brethren dearly beloved and longed for (*epipothetos*: yearned after), my joy and crown (*stephanos*: victory wreath), so stand fast in the Lord, my dearly beloved.

The closeness of Paul and the Philippian believers comes out strongly in this verse. Twice he addresses them as "dearly beloved." He yearns to be with them. His heart is further warmed as he thinks about the coming of the Lord (3:20–21), knowing that they will be part of his "victor's crown" on that day.

The progress or failure of a congregation is credited to the pastor (Revelation 2 and 3). He is held responsible for obedience or failure in presenting the Word of God to his congregation. He either shares in the gold, silver, and precious stones given to them or in the wood, hay, and stubble that is burned.

Paul knows that part of the reward he will receive in heaven will be for the maturity of the Philippian believers. Paul also speaks of this victory wreath (or crown) in relation to the Thessalonian congregation (1 Thessalonians 2:19).

A. Word Study: Crowns

In the New Testament, crowns are indicators of rewards for believers who have matured past the point of the new birth.

1. **Crown of Righteousness**: A reward for the operation of faith in the believer's life (2 Timothy 4:7–8).

2. **Crown of Joy**: A reward for believers who help other believers achieve maturity (Philippians 4:1, 1 Thessalonians 2:19).

3. **Crown of Glory**: A reward for pastors who reflect the character of Jesus Christ through the Word to their congregation (1 Peter 5:4).

4. **Crown of Life**: A reward for those who endure tremendous testing, temptations, and trials and remain faithful to the Lord (James 1:12, Revelation 2:10).

5. **Incorruptible Crown**: This is not a reward but a reference to the nature of all of the above crowns. All of our rewards in heaven are incorruptible and eternal (1 Corinthians 9:25).

B. Standing Fast in Unity

4:2 ¶ I implore Euodia and I implore Syntyche to be of the same mind in the Lord.

Euodia and Syntyche were apparently with Paul from the beginning of his ministry in Philippi as two of the many women who labored with him for the gospel in that city (Acts 16:12–15). In the beginning, they had all worked together as a team of athletes under Paul (v. 3; 1 Corinthians 9:24–27).

It is not made clear here whether their disagreement was a doctrinal issue or something else. Whatever their argument was, Paul is saying they need to come together in one mind once again.

The way to become of one mind again is "in the Lord," through the Word of God.

4:3 And I urge you also, true companion, help these women who labored with me in the gospel, with Clement also, and the rest of my fellow workers, whose names *are* in the Book of Life.

And I entreat thee also, true yokefellow, help those women which labored (*sunathleo*: strove together as a team of athletes) with me in the gospel, with Clement also, and with other my fellowlabourers, whose names are in the book of life.

Many people have speculated about the indentity of the "true companion" Paul addresses here; some say it was Luke, others say Silas, while others say it was someone else. But the person is the pastor of the church at Philippi. Paul calls on this pastor to straighten out the argument between Euodia and Syntyche. This is often the responsibility of the pastor (Titus 1:9–11).

Paul advises the pastor to call on Clement as well as other ministers in the area of Philippi. Many times, before a pastor makes a decision, he needs godly counsel from other ministers. Clement was the pastor of the church at Rome. Since Philippi was a Roman province, Clement was well known there, and he probably made frequent visits.

Apparently the pastor at Philippi also had others in his congregation who had worked with Paul in founding the church and had remained as elders and advisors. Paul and the pastor respected those other ministers as being godly men who could be counted for counsel.

C. Finding Peace While Under Pressure

4:4 ¶ Rejoice in the Lord always. Again I will say, rejoice!

The storms of life come and go, but despite our problems, rejoicing should come from our lips at all times. The voice of faith is our praise to the Lord.

Here, Paul emphatically tells the congregation to rejoice; in fact, he tells them twice! Just as praise is a choice, so the lifestyle of praise is also a choice. When the pressures of life come, it is a great temptation to forget the Christian life and all the forms of discipline which go along with it. Yet, these disciplines are even more necessary in tough times.

Paul has disciplined himself to rejoice always. He knows that praise becomes a guide in the storms of life. It helped to keep his attention on the Lord and not on the circumstances.

This rejoicing is not for the circumstances but for the promises of God which will strengthen us and will deliver us out of our circumstances. Our praise and rejoicing is for God's character, for His faithfulness and dependability which will never change.

4:5 ¶ Let your gentleness be known to all men. The Lord *is* at hand.

Let your moderation (*epieikes*: sweet reasonableness, forbearance, satis-faction with less than is your due) be known unto all men. The Lord is at hand.

The moderation Paul mentions here does not refer to sins but to our indul-gences. The world needs to see our moderation in the affairs of life. This includes everything from food, clothing, cars, and homes to entertainment and leisure activities.

Our life is to be centered on the Lord Jesus and not on things. Possessions will not get us salvation, but salvation will get us possessions. We may lose possessions, but we cannot lose the Lord Jesus. He is the greatest posses-sion we have. We are to be content with whatever we possess, knowing we can never lose the Lord Jesus (Hebrews 13:5).

We also need to look at the details of life through an awareness of the Lord's return. He is coming very soon, and possessions will mean nothing in the light of eternity. We will receive no rewards in heaven for the car we drove or the home we lived in. We will only receive rewards for what we did with the finances God entrusted us with. We will be rewarded for the souls we brought into the kingdom with our finances and the ministries we supported through our giving.

II. The 'How To' of Single-mindedness (6–9)

Paul teaches the "how to" of walking in the peace of Jesus: instead of worrying, pray; keep your mind occupied with good things; and put into practice what you have seen in God's Word.

A. Replace Worry with Prayer

> **4:6 ¶ Be anxious for nothing, but in everything by prayer and supplication, with thanksgiving, let your requests be made known to God;**

Be careful for nothing (stop worrying about even one thing) . . .

Jesus warns us about the consequences of worry in the Sermon on the Mount (Matthew 6:25–34). David and Peter agree on what we should do with all our worries: cast them over on the Lord (Psalms 55:22, 1 Peter 5:7).

In no place does the Bible say we are to worry about anything. Yet many seem to think that their worry somehow aids the plan of God. God settles everything from His side without the help of our worrying.

Worry always concerns the future. We know God has taken care of everything up until this point, but because we do not know tomorrow, we think He may fail to come through for us this time, so we worry.

God has perfect knowledge. He knows and sees the future as well as we see the past. We need to stop worrying and start trusting. God has never failed us and will not start failing us tomorrow.

. . . but in every thing by prayer (*proseuche*: worshipful prayer) and supplication (*deesis*: asking for personal needs) with thanksgiving let your requests be made known unto God.

The foundation for prayer in our lives is a relaxed attitude. Fear and worry hinder our prayers because we are saying through our attitude and actions that we do not believe the promises of God.

Instead of worrying, we need to pray over each situation. Paul instructs us to pray over everything both in worshipful prayer as well as specifically presenting our needs to God.

Such prayers need to be accompanied with thanksgiving (1 Thessalonians 5:18, 1 Timothy 2:1), which is the verbal expression of our faith.

4:7 and the peace of God, which surpasses all understanding, will guard your hearts and minds through Christ Jesus.

And (as a sure result) the peace of God, which passeth (surpasses) all (*panta*: every) understanding, shall keep (*phroureo*: to form a guard or garrison around) your hearts and minds (*noemata*: understanding) through (*en*: in) Christ Jesus.

The peace of God will replace worry once our cares are cast on the Lord. This peace comes when we realize we don't have to figure out how the result will come — that our outcome is in the hands of the Lord.

That peace of God forms a garrison to guard our minds against the wicked one's fiery darts of doubt and fear. Our emotions and thoughts will be guarded as we pull our thoughts into captivity (2 Corinthians 10:5) and keep them on the Lord and His Word.

The Word of God forms a wall of protection around the most vulnerable part of our lives: our minds. It is at the center of the war in our lives. It is the part both God and Satan desire to have and use. Both want us to think their thoughts.

B. Think on These Things

> **4:8 ¶ Finally, brethren, whatever things *are* true, whatever things *are* noble, whatever things *are* just, whatever things *are* pure, whatever things *are* lovely, whatever things *are* of good report, if *there* is any virtue and if *there* is anything praiseworthy—meditate on these things.**

Finally (in summary), brethren . . .

Paul now tells the Philippians what they are to be thinking on, now that their minds are not filled with worry. We do have power over our thoughts and do not have to let our minds wander.

1. Whatsoever things are **true** (*alethes*: sincere, the character of truth),

2. Whatsoever things are **noble** (*semnos*: worthy of reverence, dignified),

3. Whatsoever things are **just** (*dikaios*: just toward others),

4. Whatsoever things are **pure** (*hagnos*: chaste toward ourselves),

5. Whatsoever things are **lovely** (*prosphiles*: lovable, attracting love),

6. Whatsoever things are of **good report** (*euphemos*: proclaiming the best of someone),

7. If there is any **virtue** (*arête*: excellence),

8. And if there is anything **praiseworthy** (*epainos*: praiseworthy),

9. **Meditate** (*logizomai*: reflect, meditate) on these things.

When we are under pressure, our minds want to worry. When we are bored, our minds want to wander. Boredom is an enemy of the Christian life, and we need to know what to do during these times. Reflecting on the things of the Lord is important and necessary both for our stability and our continued success.

4:9 The things which you learned and received and heard and saw in me, these do, and the God of peace will be with you.

Those things, which ye have both (also) learned, and received, and heard, and seen in me, do (habitually practice): and the God of peace shall be with you.

Ultimate success in life will come as we do the Word. A believer must receive the words of Paul and learn them, hear them repeatedly, observe them being practiced in his minister's life, and finally put them into practice in his own life. Those who do these things will not only have the peace of God, but will also enjoy the presence of the one who gives peace, the God of peace.

Notice in this verse that Paul mentions hearing and observing four times more than he mentions doing. Behind every act we do for the Lord and for each other, there needs to be a lot of study, prayer, and obedience to the Word.

III. The Peace of Contentment (10–13)

After thanking the Philippians for their love offering, Paul teaches how to live free from the pressure of external circumstances.

4:10 ¶ But I rejoiced in the Lord greatly that now at last your care for me has flourished again; though you surely did care, but you lacked opportunity.

But (now) I rejoiced in the Lord greatly, that now at the last (*pote*: once more) your care (concern) of (*huper*: over) me hath flourished (*anathallo*: blossomed as trees in spring) again (once more); wherein (in which) ye were also careful (thoughtful), but ye lacked (never had an) opportunity.

The love and concern the Philippians felt for Paul flourished like plants in spring. Their love for Paul was greater now than it had ever been. Their financial giving was only an outward indicator of the growing love in their hearts.

Paul rejoiced that the Philippians had again given to his need as they had in the beginning. They had been partners with him before he had made his mistakes, and now, even though Paul had missed the Lord's will and had openly confessed this to the church, they gave again.

Paul now knows they would have given to him sooner but did not have an opportunity.

4:11 Not that I speak in regard to need, for I have learned in whatever state I am, to be content:

Not that I speak in respect of want (*husteresis*: destitution): for I have learned, in whatsoever state (circumstances) I am, therewith to be content (*autarkes*: independent of circumstance and self-sufficient).

Contentment is learned. Contentment is not a feeling or a mood. Feelings change with the circumstances while contentment comes from a heart settled on the promises of God and remains stable no matter what may occur.

The goal for every Christian is not to be freed from circumstances, but to be self-sufficient in them, knowing "If God be for us, who can be against us?" (Romans 8:31). This confidence in God can be obtained through learning, receiving, hearing, observing, and doing the Word.

Self-sufficiency combined with contentment produces confidence, but without contentment, self-sufficiency is nothing more than arrogance. Contentment is what separates the mature Christian from the sinner and carnal believer.

4:12 I know how to be abased, and I know how to abound. Everywhere and in all things I have learned both to be full and to be hungry, both to abound and to suffer need.

I know both how to be abased (*tapeinoo*: exist in lowly circumstances), and I know how to abound (*perisseuo*: have more than enough): every where (*en panti*: in everything as a whole) and in all things (*en pasin*: in all things individually) I am instructed (*mueo*: have been taught) both to be full and to be hungry, both to abound and to suffer need (*hustereo*: lack).

Paul's contentment is learned and applied in every and all situations. Paul has applied the Word equally during times of plenty and times of lack; when he had plenty of food, clothing, and shelter as well as times of hunger, thirst, and bitter cold (2 Corinthians 11:23–33). He knows none of these things can separate him from the love of God (Romans 8:35–39). It is the love of God which causes our needs to be met daily.

Paul has been instructed by the Word and by the Holy Spirit. He has put this instruction into practice in his own life and now shares these truths so we can learn also.

4:13 I can do all things through Christ who strengthens me.

I can do (*ischuo*: endowed with strength for) all things through Christ which strengtheneth (*endunamoo*: empowers) me.

In the Greek, this verse reads, "I am strong for all things in the One who constantly infuses strength in me." Paul's strength comes from his knowledge in the Word of God. Knowledge is not just stored information but something which is usable each day in our battle against the world and against satanic messengers. All of the attacks of Satan and the world are against our mind. This is why knowledge is the key to our victory (Romans 12:1–2, 2 Corinthians 10:3–5).

IV. The Fruit of Partnership (14–20)

Paul recounts the history of the partnership of the Philippians and their single-minded, united support of his ministry which will bear much fruit.

4:14 ¶ Nevertheless you have done well that you shared in my distress.

Notwithstanding ye have well done, that ye did communicate (*sugkoinoneo*: make yourself a partner) with my affliction (*thlipsis*: tribulation).

While self-sufficiency is the goal of each believer, we must always be willing to help others. Self sufficiency does not mean you only depend on God and do not receive the gifts of men. The gifts of men are the actions of God. When God supplies our need, it is not by money and provisions falling from the sky but through the hands of men (Luke 6:38).

While in his financially destitute situation, Paul was helped out by the Philippian saints who sent him a great amount of money even though they themselves faced great lack (2 Corinthians 8:1–4).

4:15 Now you Philippians know also that in the beginning of the gospel, when I departed from Macedonia, no church shared with me concerning giving and receiving but you only.

Now ye Philippians know also, that in the beginning of the gospel, when I departed from Macedonia, no church (*ekklesia*: assembly) communicated (*koinoneo*: entered into partnership) with me as concerning (*logos*: regarding an account of) giving and receiving, but ye only.

In this last mention of his partnership with the Philippians, Paul gives a brief history of the Philippian church's partnership account of giving and receiving (depositing and withdrawing) with him and his ministry. When a believer puts his money into the ministry of another believer, he shares in their rewards.

When Paul left Macedonia and ended up in Athens and then Corinth, he was broke and no longer had his friends with him. To help with the finances, he began to make tents with his newly-found companions in the ministry, Aquila and Priscilla. He did this through the week and ministered on weekends in Corinth. He could have received offerings from the Corinthian believers, but they were so touchy about money that he would rather work than offend them and keep them from receiving the Word of God.

It was during this time that the Philippians sent a large offering to Paul, allowing him to quit the tent-making business. No church came to his aid during this time except the Philippians.

Now that Paul has recovered from his detour out of the will of God, God will bless the Philippians as well as Paul because they are in partnership together. They joined with Paul during his worst time, and God is going to bless them with Paul during his best time.

4:16 For even in Thessalonica you sent *aid* once and again for my necessities.

After Paul was kicked out of Philippi, he went to Thessalonica. As he ministered there, the Philippians sent him offerings on two separate occasions.

4:17 Not that I seek the gift, but I seek the fruit that abounds to your account.

Paul was blessed by the gift the Philippians sent, but money was not what he was ultimately after. His greatest blessing was to hear the Philippians were being blessed by their generous attitude toward the gospel. Fruit (interest) that is accumulating in their spiritual account is the reward which brings joy to Paul.

4:18 Indeed I have all and abound. I am full, having received from Epaphroditus the things *sent* from you, a sweet-smelling aroma, an acceptable sacrifice, well pleasing to God.

But I have all (*panta*: all things), and abound (*perisseuo*: to the full and overflowing): I am full (*pleroo*: been filled completely), having received of Epaphroditus the things which were sent from you, an odour of a sweet smell, a sacrifice acceptable, well pleasing to God.

Because of the offering from the Philippians, Paul has more than enough natural and spiritual blessings. He has double rejoicing at this time (v. 4). The natural blessings given by the Philippians creates an abundance for Paul: he has more finances than he needs. Their generosity has also caused an overflowing spiritual joy in Paul.

The money has blessed Paul's natural life, but the attitude of love behind it blessed his spiritual life. His inward man and his outward man are both filled to overflowing.

Paul's joy was shared by the Lord Jesus. The attitude which so ministered to Paul was also a sweet-smelling aroma to the Lord. It was a sacrifice on the part of the Philippians to give to Paul because they were in such hardship at this time themselves. Their sacrifice was like the sacrifices of the Old Testament which came into the Lord's presence as sweet-smelling and acceptable to the Lord. The odor in the Lord's presence is not the money but the attitude behind the giving.

4:19 And my God shall supply all your need according to His riches in glory by Christ Jesus.

But my God shall supply (*pleroo*: fill to overflowing) all your need according to his riches (*ploutos*: wealth) in glory by Christ Jesus.

The Philippians' gift to Paul left a big deficit in their finances. But the same God who supplied for Paul in his time of need will supply for them also.

They are not to look to men but to the riches God has in glory through our mediator Christ Jesus. God uses Men to supply needs in the earth; the source is not human, but divine.

4:20 Now to our God and Father *be* glory forever and ever. Amen.

For everything we receive in life — finances or other blessings, natural or spiritual — God the Father is to receive all of the glory, honor, and thanksgiving. He is the source and eventual end of all things we have and possess.

Both Paul and the Philippians are to be giving God the glory. Paul was thanking God for what he had received. The Philippians should be thanking God for the supply which is coming. We should give God glory whether we have received blessings or are still expecting them.

All of the glory given to God will continue throughout all of eternity. One day, our possessions will be gone, and this earth will be destroyed to make way for a new one, but the Giver of all things will still be here, God Himself. He is before and will be after all things.

V. Parting Comments and Greetings (21–23)

4:21 Greet every saint in Christ Jesus. The brethren who are with me greet you.

Paul now asks for all of the members of the church at Philippi to be greeted individually. He feels such a part of each life, he wants them all to know he is doing fine and is well provided for through their gift. He also lets them know that all who are with him, those who have visited him in prison, greet the Philippian saints also.

4:22 All the saints greet you, but especially those who are of Caesar's household.

There were many in Rome who had come to know the Lord through Paul's testimony. Many of those who were born again were living in the king's palace (1:13). Paul had led them to the Lord and they were spreading the gospel to their own homes. These had never met the Philippian saints, but they knew they were part of the same household of faith and the same family of God. They didn't get to see them on earth, but they knew they would see them forever in heaven. They wanted Paul to greet the Philippian saints in his letter.

4:23 The grace of our Lord Jesus Christ be with you all. Amen.

Paul's parting comment is, of course, turning them over to the grace of God (Acts 20:32). Although he may not see them or be able to write to them again, he knows they are under a greater protection than he could ever give — God's grace.

Chapter Summary

For a believer, peace comes from single-mindedness, from eyes constantly focused on Jesus, and from God's Word.

Paul's practical instructions will, if followed, help believers to rejoice at all times, to replace worry with prayer, to think good thoughts, and to be content no matter what the circumstances.

Paul's life is proof that his teachings work. As we follow his example, we will discover a peace that passes understanding, a peace the world is looking for, a peace that will draw others to the Lord Jesus.

Paul admonishes the Philippians to continue to stand on the Word. The promises of God which have brought them to their present point of maturity will continue to take them on into the new realms of perfection God has for them (3:16).

Reference Book List

Barclay, William. 1976. *New Testament Words*. Westminster: John Knox Press.

Jamison, Robert, David Brown, and A.R. Fausset. 1997. *A Commentary on the Old and New Testaments* (3 Volume Set). Peabody, MA: Hendrickson Publishers.

Strong, James H. 1980. *Strong's Exhaustive Concordance of the Bible*, 15th ed. Nashville, TN: Abingdon Press.

Strong, James, and Joseph Thayer. 1995. *Thayers Greek-English Lexicon of the New Testament: Coded with Strong's Concordance Numbers*. Peabody, MA: Hendrickson Publishers.

Unger, Merrill. 1996. *Vine's Complete Expository Dictionary of Old and New Testament Words: With Topical Index*. Nashville, TN: Thomas Nelson.

Vincent, Marvin R. 1985. *Vincent Word Studies in the New Testament* (4 Volume Set). Peabody, MA: Hendrickson Publishers.

Wuest, Kenneth. 1980. *Word Studies from the Greek New Testament,* 2nd ed. (4 Volume Set). Grand Rapids, MI: William B. Eerdmans Publishing Company.

Zodhiates, Spiros, 1991. *The Complete Word Study New Testatment* (Word Study Series). Chatanooga, TN: AMG Publishers.

The writings of Arthur W. Pink.

The writings and audio recordings of Donald Grey Barnhouse.

Meet Bob Yandian

From 1980 to 2013, Bob Yandian was the pastor of Grace Church in his hometown of Tulsa, Oklahoma. After 33 years, he left the church to his son, Robb, with a strong and vibrant congregation. During those years, he raised up and sent out hundreds of ministers to churches and missions organizations in the United States and around the world. He has authored over thirty books and established a worldwide ministry to pastors and ministers.

He is widely acknowledged as one of the most knowledgeable Bible teachers of this generation. His practical insight and wisdom into the Word of God has helped countless people around the world to live successfully in every area of the daily Christian life.

Bob attended Southwestern College and is also a graduate of Trinity Bible College. He has served as both instructor and dean of instructors at Rhema Bible College in Broken Arrow, Oklahoma.

Bob has traveled extensively throughout the United States and internationally, taking his powerful and easy to apply teachings that bring stability and hope to hungry hearts everywhere. He is called "a pastor to pastors."

Bob and his wife, Loretta, have been married for over forty years, are parents of two married children, and have five grandchildren. Bob and Loretta Yandian reside in Tulsa, Oklahoma.

Contact Bob Yandian Ministries

Email: bym@bobyandian.com

Phone:

(918) 250-2207

Mailing Address:

Bob Yandian Ministries

PO Box 55236

Tulsa, OK 74155

www.bobyandian.com

Other Books by Bob Yandian

Calling and Separation
Decently and in Order
Faith's Destination
From Just Enough to Overflowing
God's Word to Pastors
How Deep Are the Stripes?
Leadership Secrets of David the King
Morning Moments
One Flesh
Proverbs
Spirit Controlled Life
The Bible and National Defense
Understanding End Times
Unlimited Partnership
What If the Best Is Yet to Come?
When God Is Silent
From *A New Testament Commentary* Series (sold individually or as a set):

> *Acts*
> *Colossians*
> *Ephesians*
> *Galatians*
> *James*
> *Philippians*

Fast. Easy.
Convenient.

For the latest Harrison House product information and author news, look no further than your computer. All the details on our powerful, life-changing products are just a click away. New releases, email subscriptions, testimonies, monthly specials — find them all in one place. Visit harrisonhouse.com today!

harrisonhouse.com

PRAYER OF SALVATION

God loves you — no matter who you are, no matter what your past. God loves you so much that he gave his one and only begotten Son for you. The Bible tells us that ". . . whoever believes in him shall not perish but have eternal life" (John 3:16 NIV). Jesus laid down His life and rose again so that we could spend eternity with Him and experience His absolute best on earth. If you would like to receive Jesus into your life, say the following prayer out loud and mean it in your heart.

Heavenly Father, I come to You admitting that I am a sinner. Right now, I choose to turn away from sin, and I ask You to cleanse me of all unrighteousness. I believe that Your Son, Jesus, died on the cross to take away my sins. I also believe that He rose again from the dead so that I might be forgiven of my sins and made righteous through faith in Him. I call upon the name of Jesus Christ to be the Savior and Lord of my life. Jesus, I choose to follow You and ask that You fill me with the power of the Holy Spirit. I declare that, right now, I am a child of God. I am free from sin and full of the righteousness of God. I am saved in Jesus's name. Amen.

If you prayed this prayer to receive Jesus Christ as your Savior for the first time, please contact us to receive a free book:

www.harrisonhouse.com
Harrison House
PO Box 35035
Tulsa, Oklahoma 74153